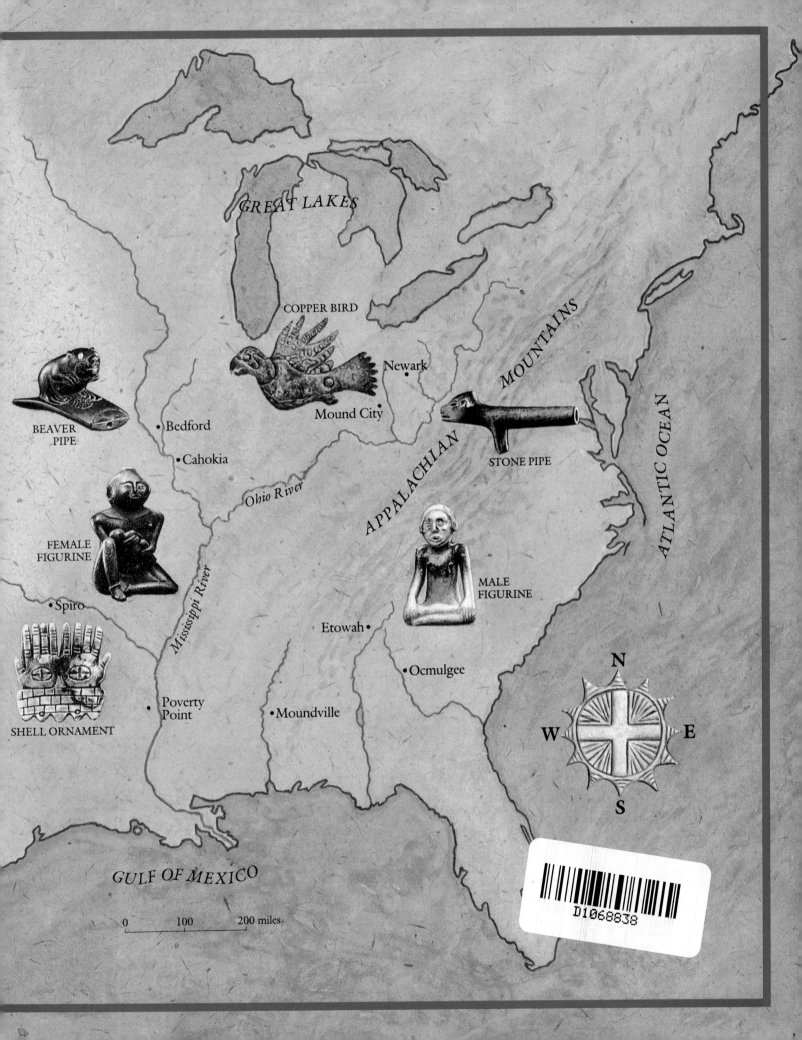

GREAT LAKES

COPPER BIRD

Newark

Mound City

BEAVER
PIPE

• Bedford

• Cahokia

Ohio River

APPALACHIAN

MOUNTAINS

STONE PIPE

ATLANTIC OCEAN

FEMALE
FIGURINE

Mississippi River

MALE
FIGURINE

• Spiro

Etowah •

SHELL ORNAMENT

• Ocmulgee

N

Poverty
Point

• Moundville

W   E

S

GULF OF MEXICO

0   100   200 miles

Cover: Carved from sandstone, this approximately 600-year-old figurine was intended to guard the bones of a high-ranking individual, perhaps a chief. Many such effigies have been found buried in the majestic temple mounds—the hallmark of the Mississippian culture. The background shows part of a 135-room cliff dwelling built around AD 1200 by the Anasazi at Betatakin, Arizona.

End paper: Painted by the artist Paul Breeden, the map encompasses the Eastern Woodlands and southwestern deserts of North America occupied by six major pre-Columbian cultures. Representative artifacts are shown near the archaeological sites in which they were discovered.

MOUND BUILDERS & CLIFF DWELLERS

Time-Life Books is a division of Time Life Inc., a wholly owned subsidary of
THE TIME INC. BOOK COMPANY

TIME-LIFE BOOKS

PRESIDENT: Mary N. Davis

MANAGING EDITOR: Thomas H. Flaherty
Director of Editorial Resources: Elise D. Ritter-Clough
Executive Art Director: Ellen Robling
Director of Photography and Research: John Conrad Weiser
Editorial Board: Dale M. Brown, Janet Cave, Roberta Conlan, Laura Foreman, Jim Hicks, Blaine Marshall, Rita Thievon Mullin, Henry Woodhead
Assistant Director of Editorial Resources/Training Manager: Norma E. Shaw

PUBLISHER: Robert H. Smith

Associate Publisher: Sandra Lafe Smith
Editorial Director: Russell B. Adams, Jr.
Marketing Director: Anne C. Everhart
Director of Production Services: Robert N. Carr
Production Manager: Prudence G. Harris
Supervisor of Quality Control: James King

Editorial Operations
Production: Celia Beattie
Library: Louise D. Forstall
Computer Composition: Deborah G. Tait (Manager), Monika D. Thayer, Janet Barnes Syring, Lillian Daniels
Interactive Media Specialist: Patti H. Cass

Library of Congress Cataloging in Publication Data
Mound Builders & Cliff Dwellers / by the editors of Time-Life Books.
    p. cm.—(Lost civilizations)
Includes bibliographical references and index.
ISBN 0-8094-9858-8 (trade)
ISBN 0-8094-9859-6 (lib. bdg.)
1. Mound builders. 2. Cliff dwellers.
3. Indians of North America—East (U.S.)—Antiquities. 4. Indians of North America—Southwest, New—Antiquities. 5. East (U.S.)—Antiquities. 6. Southwest, New—Antiquities.
I. Time-Life Books. II. Series.
E73.M68   1992
973.1—dc20   92-18534

LOST CIVILIZATIONS

SERIES EDITOR: Dale M. Brown
Series Administrator: Philip Brandt George

Editorial staff for: *Mound Builders & Cliff Dwellers*
Art Director: Barbara M. Sheppard
Picture Editor: Tina S. McDowell
Text Editors: James Lynch (principal), Charlotte Anker, Robert Somerville
Writer: Darcie Conner Johnston
Associate Editors/Research: Denise Dersin, Patricia A. Mitchell
Assistant Editor/Research: Mary Grace Mayberry
Assistant Art Director: Bill McKenney
Senior Copy Coordinator: Anne Farr
Picture Coordinator: David A. Herod
Editorial Assistant: Patricia D. Whiteford

Special Contributors: Ronald H. Bailey, Donald Dale Jackson, Norman Kolpas, Alan Lothian, Valerie Moolman (text); Paul Edholm, Aziza Meer, Eugenia S. Scharf (research); Roy Nanovic (index)

Correspondents: Elisabeth Kraemer-Singh (Bonn), Christine Hinze (London), Christina Lieberman (New York), Maria Vincenza Aloisi (Paris), Ann Natanson (Rome). Valuable assistance was also provided by: Judy Aspinall (London); Elizabeth Brown, Katheryn White (New York)

The Consultants:
Dr. Linda S. Cordell is Irvine Curator and chairperson of the Department of Anthropology at the California Academy of Sciences in San Francisco. She has directed archaeological research in New Mexico for the last 16 years and has written extensively about the Native American cultures of the Southwest.

Dr. James B. Griffin has been involved in North American archaeology since 1928, specializing in the area east of the Rocky Mountains. He is a past chairperson and professor emeritus of the Department of Anthropology at the University of Michigan. Since 1984, he has served as a research associate at the Smithsonian Institution.

Dr. Bruce D. Smith is the head of the Division of Archaeology, Anthropology at the Smithsonian's National Museum of Natural History. He has directed many field projects and authored numerous works on the Mississippian Tradition of the eastern United States.

Martha Potter Otto has conducted archaeological fieldwork over the past 30 years at numerous Adena, Hopewell, and Late Woodland sites in Ohio. She is presently the curator of archaeology at the Ohio Historical Society.

Gilbert R. Wenger worked for the National Park Service for 33 years, 14 of which he spent as Chief Archaeologist at Mesa Verde National Park. He also conducted training programs for the Utes in stabilization and interpretation of Anasazi ruins on tribal lands.

Other Publications:
THE AMERICAN INDIANS
THE ART OF WOODWORKING
ECHOES OF GLORY
THE NEW FACE OF WAR
HOW THINGS WORK
WINGS OF WAR
CREATIVE EVERYDAY COOKING
COLLECTOR'S LIBRARY OF THE UNKNOWN
CLASSICS OF WORLD WAR II
TIME-LIFE LIBRARY OF CURIOUS AND UNUSUAL FACTS
AMERICAN COUNTRY
VOYAGE THROUGH THE UNIVERSE
THE THIRD REICH
THE TIME-LIFE GARDENER'S GUIDE
MYSTERIES OF THE UNKNOWN
TIME FRAME
FIX IT YOURSELF
FITNESS, HEALTH & NUTRITION
SUCCESSFUL PARENTING
HEALTHY HOME COOKING
UNDERSTANDING COMPUTERS
LIBRARY OF NATIONS
THE ENCHANTED WORLD
THE KODAK LIBRARY OF CREATIVE PHOTOGRAPHY
GREAT MEALS IN MINUTES
THE CIVIL WAR
PLANET EARTH
COLLECTOR'S LIBRARY OF THE CIVIL WAR
THE EPIC OF FLIGHT
THE GOOD COOK
WORLD WAR II
HOME REPAIR AND IMPROVEMENT
THE OLD WEST

For information on and a full description of any of the Time-Life Books series listed above, please call 1-800-621-7026 or write:
Reader Information
Time-Life Customer Service
P.O. Box C-32068
Richmond, Virginia 23261-2068

This volume is one in a series that explores the worlds of the past, using the finds of archaeologists and other scientists to bring ancient peoples and their cultures vividly to life.

Other volumes include:

Egypt: Land of the Pharaohs
Aztecs: Reign of Blood & Splendor
Pompeii: The Vanished City
Incas: Lords of Gold and Glory
The Holy Land

MOUND BUILDERS & CLIFF DWELLERS

By the Editors of Time-Life Books

TIME-LIFE BOOKS, ALEXANDRIA, VIRGINIA

CONTENTS

THE ADENA AND THE HOPEWELL: A MONUMENTAL HERITAGE

In a hand-tinted photograph, this 2,000-year-old earthen mound rising from the south central Ohio landscape covers burials of the Hopewell, ancient inhabitants of the region. The site forms part of a 13-acre Indian necropolis dubbed Mound City.

It was an eerie experience," recalled Warren Cremer of his helicopter flight over Arizona's Coconino National Forest late on a summer afternoon in 1991. Cremer loved to roam Coconino's 1.8 million acres, a starkly beautiful and surprisingly diverse mix of canyon, desert, lofty pine-clad mountains, and alpine tundra. Within its boundaries lay thousands of prehistoric ruins left by Native Americans who once inhabited the region, and it was an elusive relic from these long-departed residents that made Cremer's excursion this day so unforgettable.

With the light rapidly fading, the helicopter pilot agreed to one final pass around a 1,200-foot-high red sandstone butte that sheltered an ancient multistory stone dwelling perched a third of the way up the sheer rockface. Suddenly, on a ledge some 600 feet above this cliff house, Cremer glimpsed the mouth of a cave directly in front of him. Silhouetted against the dark opening, catching the setting sun's last rays, three enormous pottery vessels could be seen.

He knew at once he had chanced upon something sensational. "The pots had been sitting there for maybe 700 years," he noted with awe. "But the cave was situated so that you couldn't see it either from the ground or from the crown of the butte 200 feet above. I came within 150 yards of it five years ago and had no idea it was there. We wouldn't have seen it from the helicopter at any other time of day—

the light just happened to be right." Cremer alerted Coconino headquarters straightaway.

Soon, a group of archaeologists equipped with ropes and ladders made their way up the cliff and inspected the site. In addition to the cluster of three reddish brown unglazed vessels at the entrance, the cave contained two more pots, together with baskets and other artifacts. The scientists quickly realized that they were the first to enter the site since its abandonment centuries before. In fact, one of the archaeologists, Peter Pilles, said he felt as though he had "jumped into someone's kitchen while the person was away."

Though it hardly constituted a treasure trove in the pecuniary sense, Pilles deemed the cache "of exceptional importance." The clay jars, with a capacity of up to 30 gallons, were among the largest intact prehistoric vessels ever found in Arizona. They had almost certainly belonged to the occupants of the six-room cliff house far below, who probably used the cave as a pantry or storage room and the jars for storing precious water.

The team of experts recognized the pottery as a type called Tuzigoot Plain and confirmed that it had been fashioned sometime between AD 1250 and 1350 by the Sinagua Indians. Researchers hope that analysis of the ancient residue in the vessels and in the cave

At the moment of discovery in 1991, a passenger aboard a helicopter touring Arizona's Coconino National Forest snapped the photograph at top of three large ceramic pots in the mouth of a previously unknown cliffside cave, where they had perched untouched for about 700 years. Scientists exploring the cave, including U.S. archaeologist Peter Pilles (above), *identified the vessels and a variety of other domestic artifacts found there as belonging to the Sinagua Indians, who departed the area around AD 1400.*

itself will yield new clues to the Sinagua way of life. The Sinagua, whose name in Spanish means "without water," used an array of dryland farming techniques to coax a harvest from the stingy, arid land, cultivating beans, corn, and squash. Carrying on a brisk exchange of goods and ideas with neighboring cultures, they flourished around present-day Flagstaff for nearly eight centuries.

Then, around 1400, the Sinagua abandoned their high-up homes—for reasons still not agreed upon—and melded into other surrounding communities. To say that they disappeared would be a canard, for their bloodlines endure in the present-day Indian tribes of the region. Nevertheless, the Sinagua, as a distinct cultural entity, faded into oblivion long before Columbus "discovered" America, leaving archaeologists to puzzle out the reasons for their rise and fall.

The Sinagua are but one of a long list of Native American cultures that sprouted, blossomed, and then withered away before European settlers arrived to claim the "New World" as their own domain. These prehistoric societies left no written records of their achievements, cultural practices, religious beliefs, or everyday life. It is not even known what they called themselves. Consequently, archaeologists have bestowed names descriptive of each culture's environment—like Sinagua—or associated with a particular site rich in artifacts.

Fortunately, physical evidence of these astonishingly diverse cultures has survived, much of it monumental in size and compelling for what it suggests about their power and organizational ability. But smaller remains have their own fascinating stories to impart. Shards of pottery, baskets, jewelry, human bones, spearpoints chipped from stone, seeds, pollen—even the congealed leftovers of meals cooked and eaten many centuries ago—provide clues that help the scientist-cum-detective assemble a more intimate portrait of the real people behind the disembodied artifacts.

But it does not require a contemporary specialist in ancient civilizations to realize that the landmass of the present-day United States harbored a broad spectrum of highly sophisticated pre-Columbian societies. They were most spectacularly there. As early as the 16th century, Spanish treasure hunters such as Hernando de Soto in the Southeast and Francisco de Coronado in the Southwest encountered both the ancient, abandoned traces of once-thriving settlements and the living tribes whose ancestors had created them. But the conquistadors' interest lay in gold, not in scientific exploration, and they left empty-handed.

Two centuries later, however, waves of European immigrants flooded westward from the Atlantic seaboard into what they thought was a virgin wilderness. Instead, they found evidence of widespread habitation—far greater than could be accounted for by the limited numbers of Indians living in the area. Massive earthworks of every description—pyramids, cones, hillocks, terraced platforms, and animal shapes that had taken thousands of man-hours to construct—dotted the landscape west of the Appalachian Mountains. Their exact number can never be ascertained since a great many were lost to the farmer's plow, river erosion, and burgeoning townships before any sort of tally could be undertaken, but it is no exaggeration to say that there were hundreds of thousands of them. Indeed, prehistoric America contained many more pyramids than did the Egypt of the pharaohs; one—still standing in the state of Illinois—even had a larger base circumference than that of the Great Pyramid of Khufu. Around this earthen ceremonial center in the 1100s lay a bustling city of 12,000 inhabitants, roughly the population of London at that time, with links to other settlements scattered hundreds of miles beyond its wooden palisades.

Subsequently, when pioneers reached the dry southwestern environs of the continent, they found dazzling evidence of other, very different cultures that had created many of their greatest masterpieces in stone rather than soil. Objects of wood, leather, cloth, and feathers that would have rotted away in the moister climate of the eastern woodlands survived intact here to amaze with the intricacy and beauty of their execution. Remaining sections of irrigation canals suggested another kind of technical achievement, a sign that the surrounding desert had once bloomed under someone's skillful hand.

Later archaeological investigations would show that these same farmers were also preeminent artists who, among other things, had produced some of the world's most beautiful pottery and, in another expression of their creativity, come up with the rudiments of etching at least four centuries before Renaissance Europe developed the technique. The region's predominant culture, which came to be known as the Anasazi, left its mark on so many locales, and over so wide an area, that its remains are still being discovered and cataloged today. Among their most captivating feats was the construction of vertiginous cliff dwellings and a breathtaking, five-story, 800-room

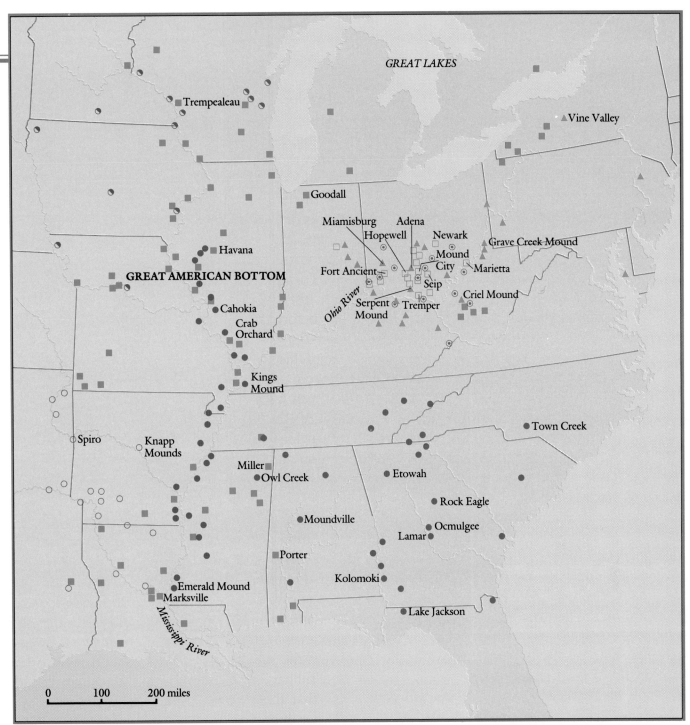

GREAT LAKES

Vine Valley

Trempealeau

Goodall

Miamisburg   Adena
Hopewell   Newark
Grave Creek Mound

Havana

Mound
City   Marietta

GREAT AMERICAN BOTTOM

Fort Ancient

Ohio River

Seip

Cahokia

Serpent   Tremper
Mound

Criel Mound

Crab
Orchard

Kings
Mound

Town Creek

Spiro

Knapp
Mounds

Miller
Owl Creek

Etowah

Rock Eagle

Moundville

Ocmulgee

Lamar

Porter

Kolomoki

Emerald Mound
Marksville

Lake Jackson

Mississippi River

0   100   200 miles

▲ *Adena sites*
■ *Hopewell sites*
□ *Ohio Hopewell sites*
● *Mississippian sites*
○ *Caddoan Mississippian sites*
◑ *Oneota Mississippian sites*
◉ *Fort Ancient sites*

This map shows regions of the eastern United States in which three separate groups of Mound Builders—represented by different colors and symbols—flourished over the span of two millennia. Because of the abundant natural resources and easily tilled soils, their settlements clustered in river-valley settings. From 500 BC to the first century AD, the Adena (green) resided in the central Ohio River valley, spreading their influence

from southeastern Indiana to southwestern Pennsylvania. The Hopewell (red), whose culture peaked between 50 BC and AD 400, centered in Ohio as well, although they obtained goods and raw materials from many regions of the continental United States. From AD 800 to the European invasion, the Mississippians (blue)—builders of the great temple mounds—thrived along the Mississippi and its tributaries and in the Southeast.

Outlined with lime for visibility, this effigy mound in northeastern Iowa reveals its bear form most clearly from the air. It is one of many animal-shaped earthworks scattered across Iowa, Wisconsin, and Minnesota that were built sometime between AD 650 and 1200. Like the bear, the nearby conical and linear mounds may have fulfilled a symbolic as well as a funerary purpose.

complex from the 12th century that would retain the title of largest apartment house in the world until the 1880s.

Like the man-made wonders of the Southwest, the myriad earthen legacies of the eastern United States would inspire in the young country's citizens the kind of amazement evinced by the temples, palaces, and ruins of the Old World. In 1848, a newspaper editor wrote of one such array of mounds and embankments in Newark, Ohio: "In entering the ancient avenue for the first time, the visitor does not fail to experience a sensation of awe, such as he might feel in passing the portals of an Egyptian temple."

To the pioneers, the region west of the Alleghenies, with its web of pristine rivers, fertile bottom lands, and unending forests, seemed at first to be practically unsullied by human habitation except for an occasional band of roving Indians. But as the settlers pushed into the Middle West during the late 18th century, they were astonished to find earthwork after earthwork rearing ahead of them, ranging from small conical mounds to elaborate compounds of ramparts and embankments that covered up to 200 acres. The earthen monuments, the product of one of the most concerted human endeavors ever, were heavily concentrated in the Ohio Valley, which alone contained an estimated 10,000. But, as soon became clear, the works also stretched from Canada and western New York to Nebraska and along the Gulf coast from Florida to eastern Texas.

These tumuli aroused the curiosity of the early settlers. Some had been built in the shape of birds, beasts, or serpents. Others took such geometric forms as octagons, circles, and squares; still others resembled truncated pyramids, with deliberately flattened tops. Hilltop complexes, akin to forts with their thick walls and ramparts, seemed to stand mute guard against long-forgotten enemies.

Intrigued farmers jabbed shovels into some of the earthworks and found nothing. But not all of the mounds proved barren of booty; many—especially the conical ones—yielded pottery, tools, weapons, jewelry, and human remains. The goods obviously were

In an Iowa forest on the edge of a farm field, a large earthwork portrays a bird in flight. Most of the birds, bears, and stylized lizards fashioned by the effigy-makers rise only about three feet high but stretch up to 100 feet in length.

meant to accompany the deceased on their journey into the afterlife.

One of the most careful of the early shovel wielders was that renaissance man Thomas Jefferson. Sometime before 1781, the indefatigable Virginia statesman, architect, and scientist undertook the excavation of a small burial mound near his home, Monticello. His techniques anticipated the methods of professional archaeologists more than a century later. He first dug a trial trench in order to gain a preliminary understanding of the mound's structure, paying close attention to the stratification of the human bones he unearthed. The remains lay jumbled about in such confusion, he wrote, "as to give the idea of bones emptied promiscuously from a bag or basket." He conjectured that the mound might contain as many as a thousand skeletons, but whose? Jefferson, a student of Indian lore since boyhood, had no doubt that this and other Virginia mounds were the work of American Indians.

While some of Jefferson's countrymen agreed that Indians could have built the mounds in Virginia or those farther west, most discounted the notion. Many of the works were staggering in size and would have required droves of highly organized laborers to construct. Most settlers of the Ohio Valley regarded the former tenants of the land with disdain and in their prejudice concluded that they lacked the ambition and skill to undertake such enormous engineering projects.

At the same time, one man's innovative application of old forest lore demonstrated that the mounds were too ancient to be the work of the contemporary Indians' immediate ancestors. Manasseh Cutler, an astute clergyman from Massachusetts, arrived at the new settlement of Marietta on the Ohio River in 1788 and found trees being felled on a 40-acre mound complex. He logically assumed the trees would have flourished only after the site had been abandoned. Know-

Attracting curious sightseers ever since its discovery by 18th-century frontier travelers, imposing Grave Creek Mound at Moundsville, West Virginia, stands almost 70 feet high in what was once a grand complex of Adena and Hopewell mounds and earthworks. Measuring 240 feet across, the symmetrical cone was built with the dumping of some three million basketloads—or 57,000 tons—of soil. It is seen below in an engraving published in 1848.

Ten years earlier, Abelard Tomlinson, the proprietor of what was then called Mammoth Mound, conducted its first excavation, sinking a shaft through the top and discovering two log tombs on the way down, one con-

taining great quantities of copper, shell, and mica ornaments among the human bones. Subsequent digs, in which several other burials came to light, indisputably marked the mound as late Adena.

However, Grave Creek was once perhaps more famous—or infamous—for a small oval of sandstone *(below)* that Tomlinson claimed to have pulled from the dirt in 1838. Bearing a mysterious 25-character inscription, the tablet generated 35 years of controversy as experts variously identified the alphabet as Celtic, Etruscan, Canaanite, Numidian, Old Gaelic, and Phoenician, to name but a few. One philologist, attempting to translate the message, claimed it told of assassination; another propounded a preposterous "Thou shinest in thy impetuous clan and rapid chamois." Ultimately, the tablet would be dismissed as a fraud.

Capitalizing on the mound's

appeal, entrepreneurs have at various times set up a museum inside an excavation shaft, built a saloon on the summit, and run a racetrack around the base. Today the monument is preserved as the primary feature at Grave Creek State Park.

ing that the age of trees could be determined by the number of annual growth rings in a cross section of the trunk, he concluded that the mounds were anywhere from 400 to 1,000 years old. Although he erred in the precise age, the clergyman's study was scientifically sound for its time and probably constituted the first archaeological application of tree-ring dating—the embryonic science of dendrochronology *(pages 90-91)*.

By the early 19th century, a fable regarding the mound builders had taken root in the young American imagination. Rejecting out of hand the possibility that mere Indians had built the earthworks, the mythmakers invoked a superior prehistoric race now vanished from the plains and river valleys where the monuments stood. Scholars and laymen, probing ancient texts as well as their own fecund imaginations, attributed the mounds to a dizzying array of ancient peoples, from Vikings and Anglo-Saxons to Greeks, Romans, Persians, Phoenicians, and even the storied Ten Lost Tribes of Israel—practically anyone in the Old World, in fact, who had ever built a mound or whose texts referred to creating "high places"—anyone except the Indians.

Although some versions of the vanished-race notion had the mound builders migrating to Mexico to found advanced civilizations there, most depicted a livelier denouement. The mound builders were destroyed, many writers suggested, by barbarous American Indians. In his 1832 poem "The Prairies," William Cullen Bryant wrote, "The red man came—The roaming hunter tribes, warlike and fierce, And the Mound-Builders vanished from the earth. . . . All is gone; All—save the piles of earth that hold their bones."

The fascination with mounds led to numerous studies that, while nonetheless feeding the myth, helped lay the foundations of modern American archaeology. In the Ohio settlement of Circleville—so named for the two concentric earthworks attached to a square enclosure upon which the town sat—the postmaster, Caleb Atwater, proved himself a superb amateur archaeologist. Even as many mounds around the state were disappearing under the farmer's plow, Atwater systematically studied, measured, and mapped the ones that survived, then published his detailed descriptions in 1820.

But if Atwater was a careful and methodical surveyor of the mounds, he also tended to wax romantic in accounting for their origins. Atwater concluded that the mound builders had come from India, in part because the people of that country had established their sacred places on the banks of rivers. To buttress this conclusion, he misinterpreted a clay pot discovered in a mound in Tennessee as a three-headed idol representing a triumvirate of gods worshiped in India. Although his theory appears foolish from a contemporary perspective, experts like Stephen Williams of Harvard, one of the leading authorities on the mounds, laud Atwater for the breadth of his examinations and the diligence with which he pursued them.

A decade later in Philadelphia, the distinguished physician Samuel G. Morton began studying the skulls of the mound builders. In an attempt to determine if there were any differences in cranial capacity based on race, Morton assembled a collection of 968 human skulls for his investigations. A pioneer in physical anthropology, he devised 10 different techniques for analyzing a skull, including filling it with mustard seeds to determine its volume.

Comparing eight skulls excavated from mounds with six skulls known to belong to contemporary Indians, he concluded—rightly, though from a vastly oversimplified reliance on cranial configuration—that they belonged to the same race. However, presenting this evidence in his 1839 book *Crania Americana,* Morton stumbled and fit his facts to the prevailing myth. Mound builders and Indians were a single race, he averred, but one that encompassed two branches: the civilized Toltecan, named after the early inhabitants of Mexico whom the Aztecs had greatly admired, and the Barbarous. Naturally, he relegated the Indians to the second category.

During the following decade, a pair of remarkable amateurs completed a landmark study back in the heart of the mound country. Working out of Chillicothe, Ohio, under the auspices of the American Ethnological Society, Ephraim G. Squier, a local newspaper editor, and Edwin H. Davis, a physician, explored more than 200 mounds and 100 earthen enclosures between 1845 and 1847. They excavated the nearby necropolis of Mound City—a 13-acre site containing 23 burial mounds—all the while keeping track of the levels bearing pottery, ornaments, and other artifacts. They surveyed earthworks, prepared and obtained detailed drawings and contour maps, and critically assessed the work of Caleb Atwater and other researchers. "At the outset," Squier said, "all preconceived notions were abandoned, and the work of research commenced, as if no speculations had been indulged in, nor anything before been known."

Squier and Davis published their findings in 1848 as the first volume in a series of books on natural science sponsored by the recently established Smithsonian Institution. Their results anticipated the ideas of modern archaeologists with astonishing prescience. They referred, for example, to the geometric earthworks as "sacred enclosures" devoted to religious functions, and surmised that the builders were skilled engineers and mathematicians.

The drawings proved invaluable because so many of the earthworks have since disappeared. These precisely and elegantly rendered images *(pages 34-40)* are prominently displayed at surviving mounds in Ohio as guides for visitors. Squier and Davis's book, *Ancient Monuments of the Mississippi Valley,* won such widespread attention that, in 1849, the newly elected president, Zachary Taylor, appointed Squier, a political activist, to a diplomatic post in Central America, where he continued to pursue his archaeological interests.

For all that, the erroneous myth of the "Mound-Builders" endured and flourished. Even Squier concluded that the earthworks displayed "a degree of knowledge much superior to that known to have been possessed by the hunter tribes of North America." The pottery and other art unearthed from the mounds far exceeded the "clumsy and ungraceful" production of Indians—whom he labeled "those hostile savage hordes."

Enlightened men and just plain folks debated the issue until nearly the end of the century. The majority still came down on the side of J. W. Foster, an eminent geologist and the president of the Chicago Academy of Sciences, who clung to the myth. To suppose that the Indians, a people "signalized by treachery and cruelty," had created the mounds, Foster wrote in 1873, "is as preposterous, almost, as to suppose that they built the pyramids of Egypt."

Finally, two powerful trendsetters in the American scientific community proved instrumental in finally promoting the truth. John Wesley Powell—a Civil War veteran whose heroic expedition through the Grand Canyon in 1869 had led to his appointment in 1875 as director of the U.S. Geological Survey—joined forces with the Smithsonian Institution. A passionate student of the American Indian, Powell lobbied for the creation of the Smithsonian's Bureau of Ethnology in 1879. He became its chief, serving there as well as directing the Geological Survey until his death in 1902.

Powell wanted the Bureau of Ethnology to conduct research, as its name implied, on existing tribes rather than probe recondite archaeological controversies. Growing up around mounds in Ohio, Wisconsin, and Illinois, he had dug in them—and had also studied contemporary Indian cultures. He had little doubt that the mounds had been created by the forerunners of these Indians. When pressure from archaeologists pushed Congress to appropriate $5,000 for the bureau to investigate the mounds, he seized the opportunity to resolve the issue and get on with more productive studies.

In late 1881, Powell appointed Cyrus Thomas to head the bureau's Division of Mound Exploration and instructed him to answer the direct question, "Were the mounds built by the Indians?" Powell thought he already knew the answer, but then so did Thomas, a man of the old school, who described himself as "a pronounced believer in the existence of a race of Mound Builders, distinct from the American Indians." But Thomas, a former lawyer, school administrator, evangelical minister, science professor, and entomologist, did not, to his credit, allow his prejudice to overwhelm him. He cast aside preconceived notions in his effort to unearth the facts. Even as he began work, a popular book by the former Minnesota congressman Ignatius Donnelly confidently announced that the mound builders were actually survivors of the lost continent of Atlantis.

Lacking funds and manpower to survey and excavate all the mounds and fearing that many would soon be plundered or otherwise destroyed, Thomas hit upon a workable compromise. He ordered the detailed examination of representative mounds in several different regions at the same time. At the peak of operations, he had six assistants at work in eight far-flung states from Florida to the Dakotas. A stern and tight-fisted taskmaster, he based pay on performance and even slashed the wages of a relative who submitted a sloppy report. Prodded by Thomas to keep moving and produce, his investigators eventually explored more than 2,000 mounds in 24 different states and obtained 40,000 artifacts—most of this, amazingly enough, during a four-year period.

In his long-awaited, 730-page final report published in 1894, Thomas wrote that the myth had become so powerful, "that once it has taken possession of the mind it warps and biases all its investigations and conclusions." But not this one: In exhaustive detail, Thomas demonstrated that widely differing types of mounds had to have been built by different cultures at different times and that

RECORDERS OF A VANISHED SPLENDOR

Almost immediately after 23-year-old journalist Ephraim Squier migrated from New York to Chillicothe, Ohio, in early 1845, he joined forces with local physician Edwin Davis, 10 years his senior and an amateur archaeologist. Over the next two years they explored some 200 mounds and 100 earthworks, detailing their findings in a volume entitled *Ancient Monuments of the Mississippi Valley*. Published by the Smithsonian in 1848, this opus is an invaluable record of many monuments that were later lost to development.

Davis financed their work and undertook the preservation of many of the several thousand artifacts they unearthed; Squier prepared surveys, made drawings of the sites, and tended to publication arrangements. But they disagreed over the crediting of their respective contributions, and ultimately Davis, believing the artifacts to be his, sold most of his collection to an Englishman for $10,000, after a fruitless hunt for an American buyer. The pieces are now in the British Museum.

EPHRAIM G. SQUIER
EDWIN H. DAVIS

mound building went on in the Southeast even after the European conquest. "The links directly connecting the Indians and the mound builders are so numerous and well established," he concluded, "that there should be no longer any hesitancy in accepting the theory that they are one and the same people."

The Smithsonian survey, along with other professional efforts, helped explode the myth; but the mystery of precisely who built the mounds and why still remained largely unsolved. Over the past century, archaeologists have sought the solution by deciphering, piece by piece, fragment by fragment, the unwritten record of the Mound Builders and their predecessors. This project, massive and ongoing, has provided a more coherent portrait of their history filled with many fascinating details, but one that is still missing major components.

That history began at least 15,000 years ago, toward the end of the last Ice Age, when the first American immigrants crossed from Siberia into Alaska on a temporary, marshy land bridge and ventured south between the glaciers, hunting herds of mammoths and other big game until much of it became extinct, about 10,000 years ago. They and their successors pursued smaller game, fished, and foraged for wild plants. By about 1000 BC, various groups in the eastern part of North America had achieved three prerequisites crucial to the development of culture: They made pottery, practiced rudimentary agriculture, and devoted much care and ceremony to the burial of their dead, placing them in kames—gravelly deposits left by receding glaciers—and other natural ridges and mounds.

Over time, the early Indians began actually constructing mounds for their dead instead of relying on natural formations. The first of the major mound-building cultures, the Adena, appeared around 500 BC in the central Ohio Valley. Archaeologists borrowed the name from an estate near Chillicothe, Ohio, where a mound containing distinctive artifacts was excavated in 1901. Though focused on an area within a 150-mile radius of Chillicothe and the Scioto River, their imprint on the land extended into western Pennsylvania, West Virginia, northern Kentucky, and southeastern Indiana.

An extensive program of government-sponsored excavations—mostly in Kentucky—during the Great Depression of the 1930s helped unearth evidence of a variety of Adena mortuary practices. The Adena cremated some of their dead. Others they stretched

19

out for burial in temporary graves, or possibly left exposed in trees or on ceremonial platforms to decay and be fed upon by birds of prey so that the bare bones could then be bundled together for burial.

Interment also varied. Early in their history, the Adena dug a shallow pit for the corpse, lined it with clay or bark, and heaped up dirt of different types—for unknown symbolic reasons—to form a low mound comprising a mottled patchwork of soil colors. Later they constructed elaborate, log-lined tombs, sometimes with a log roof and containing more than one body, then covered the structures with earth. Occasionally, circular wooden houses surrounded the log tombs. The corpse may have lain in state for many days, lavished with red ocher and other pigments that would have given it the blush of life, and attended with great ceremony. Then, presumably as climax to the long ritual, the house was torn down and covered with earth.

The most elaborate burials may have been reserved for what Charles E. Snow, the late expert on Adena physiology, called "the honored dead." He believed that cremation was for the common people, log-tomb burial for the aristocracy. The increasing complexity of the interment—and the higher quality of the artifacts accompanying it—suggest that social distinctions became more sharply defined over time. Interestingly, the highest-ranking individuals may also have been the tallest. Among the males of the honored dead, Snow believed, a height of six feet was not uncommon.

Many Adena mounds contain multiple layers, having gradually expanded as burials were added to them over the centuries. The Cresap Mound on the Ohio River, six miles south of the aptly named Moundsville, West Virginia, exhibits such incremental growth. In the summer of 1958, Don W. Dragoo of Pittsburgh's Carnegie Museum excavated Cresap in a salvage operation: A coal company had purchased the land for an industrial plant. The company agreed to assist by providing four workers and power machinery to carry away the soil. To safeguard the mound's contents, however, the diggers used hand-held hoes and small trowels, biting off an inch or so of soil at a time and contending all the while with the roots of a locust tree perched atop the summit. Though the mound was relatively small—15 feet high and about 70 feet in diameter at the base—the job took 13 weeks, more than twice what Dragoo had projected.

It was worth it. Dragoo found the skeletons of at least 54 persons interred in three major concentrations, from 3.3 feet below the mound floor to 13.5 feet above it. Posts, which left an indelible record in the clay after they rotted away, and the remains of a hearth indicated that the mound had been constructed around a pre-existing, dismantled house. Burials had been going on here for at least two centuries, from about 200 BC to AD 50, and had ranged from simple, shallow pits to log structures. By carefully recording the layers and studying the finds they revealed, Dragoo could piece together a clearer picture of the stages of Adena development. "I was at last presented with the previously missing key to Adena chronology," Dragoo reported. "Scraps of information that meant little before now took on new meaning." This one mound provided a sequential history of Adena burial practices in microcosm, underscoring a growing sophistication. Grave artifacts from the mound's

Forty-five miles north of St. Louis, Missouri, where the Mississippi and Illinois rivers converge, scientists and students explore the Koster Site, named for the farmer who owned the land. Digging down to a depth of 34 feet, excavators have uncovered 14 separate episodes of habitation, called horizons. With most predating the Adena and Hopewell, the levels stretch back 8,000 years.

base consisted of chipped stone tools and scrapers, bone awls, and other utilitarian items. Later—and higher—levels contained stone pendants, bracelets, and finger rings made of copper, ornamental silhouettes cut from the crystalline rock known as mica that readily separates into thin sheets, and other goods that would have been suitable grave accompaniments only for revered members of the community. An upper layer of Cresap Mound even contained a so-called trophy skull—a slightly polished specimen, perhaps that of a conquered enemy or an honored ancestor—perched on the lap of a skeleton.

Other mounds elsewhere yielded fascinating artifacts that probably served as ceremonial objects for the Adena religion. A headdress made from the skullcap and antlers of an actual deer or elk may have allowed a shaman, or holy man, to impersonate this animal. That shamans acted out fiercer roles was suggested by the upper jaw of a wolf discovered in Kentucky's Wright Mound around 1940 by the respected Adena authority William S. Webb. The wolf's palate bone had been trimmed to a spatula shape—evidently to serve as a kind of handle—with the incisors still in place. Nearly two decades later, Webb confirmed his suspicion that it may have been worn in the mouth as a mask. Researchers excavating the Ayers Mound in Kentucky found a similar wolf jaw next to the skull of an adult male, possibly a shaman. The man's upper lateral and medial incisor teeth were missing, allowing the insertion of the wolf palate into his mouth.

In this instance, the connection between the wolf mask and the man with the mutilated mouth seems solid, but archaeologists

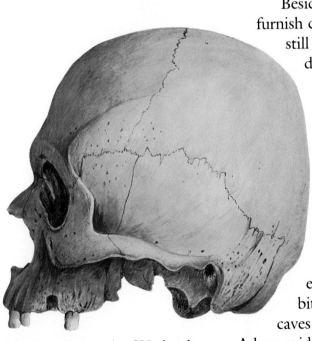

seldom can be so certain about who once owned the artifacts. A good example is that highly distinctive Adena ceremonial item, the smoking pipe. A man's pipe accompanied him to the grave, presumably to serve him in the afterlife. But as Don Dragoo has pointed out, no fewer than 32 pipes were found with one individual in one mound. "Why?" he asks. "Was this man the pipemaker? Was this a way of paying tribute to a revered individual in which the men of the clan gave up their prized pipes? Did only certain individuals have the right to a pipe?" Questions like these constantly vex archaeologists studying the early Indian cultures, but, as Dragoo says, "unfortunately, all too often the available information is insufficient to warrant positive answers."

Besides providing bones and artifacts, burial mounds also furnish clues about the nature of Adena structures. For reasons still unclear, mounds frequently arose on the sites of torn-down houses. When excavated, postholes from these structures reveal circular floor plans ranging in diameter from 15 feet to 60 feet. The largest buildings may have served as ritual gathering places. The 11-degree angle of the postholes indicates that the walls tilted slightly outward under a thatched or bark roof, probably to prevent water from running down the sides and rotting the slabs of bark lashed to the posts.

In turn, the remains of dwelling places help sketch in other fragments of how the Adena lived. Hearths of these vanished houses yield carbonized pieces of nutshells, discarded animal bones, and centuries-old bits of food. In addition, the dry conditions in some of the caves and rock shelters in Kentucky and Ohio, where some Adena evidently lived for part of the year, have preserved seeds and fecal matter. Examined and analyzed, these remains reveal a people who hunted deer, elk, and small game, gathered wild plants and nuts, and practiced rudimentary farming that enabled them to grow gourds and sunflowers.

One of the most striking and best-known earthworks in the United States—the Great Serpent Mound, which writhes across a ridge in southwestern Ohio—is often attributed to the Adena, although, as is frequently the case with this long-defunct culture, schol-

Like the ancient peoples of Mexico, the Adena typically carried their infants on cradleboards, strapping the tiny heads to the tote to keep their weak necks from snapping, as is illustrated at left with a child's skull, a cradleboard, and textiles found separately at an Adena site in Kentucky. This custom permanently flattened the back of the head, as is shown in Squier and Davis drawings that compare an adult skull deformed by the practice (above) with one that was not (top).

ars cannot say for certain that they built it. The grass-covered, undulating figure—20 feet wide and five feet high—would, if fully uncoiled, stretch for nearly a quarter of a mile from its tightly wound tail to its gaping mouth. It is the largest known snake effigy in the world. "Was this a symbol of the old serpent faith, here on the western continent?" asked Fredric Ward Putnam, the director of Harvard's Peabody Museum, in 1890, who, visiting the site, found himself in a mood for a little reflection. "Reclining on one of the huge folds of this gigantic serpent, as the last rays of the sun, glancing from distant hilltops, cast their long shadows over the valley, I mused on the probabilities of the past; and there seemed to come to me a picture as of a distant time, and with it came a demand for an interpretation of this mystery. The unknown must become known."

To preserve the mound, Putnam raised $5,880 from private donors in Boston. In 1900, Harvard deeded the 60-acre site to the state of Ohio. Now a public park, the Serpent Mound attracts thou-

Engraved with mirror images of stylized birds of prey, the Wilmington tablet —a 4-by-5-inch pallet of sandstone found in Clinton County, Ohio—may have been used by the Adena for tattooing, or for stamping cloth or walls. The back side is grooved in the manner of a whetstone, indicating that bone needles or knives were sharpened there, and is embedded with red ocher, which was used as a body paint. The incised tablet is one of only 14 known to exist.

sands of visitors every year—and no end of speculation. The enigmatic oval near the snake's head, variously defined as a frog or an egg about to be swallowed or the open mouth of the snake as it strikes, piques the curiosity of all who view it.

The gradual change in the Adena around the last century BC—like so much else about them—remains a mystery. Some five centuries after their appearance, the Adena culture in Ohio apparently metamorphosed gradually into a succeeding mound-builder culture, now known as the Hopewell after the Ohio farm where some artifacts were first unearthed. The Hopewell appear to have continued and elaborated burial practices and other customs inherited from the Adena, but they eventually developed to an unprecedented level, achieving a dazzling florescence that dimmed the formidable attainments of their predecessors.

The Hopewell carried Adena proficiencies to new heights. They fashioned metal and stone into ornaments of surpassing beauty. In contrast to the simple circular embankments that sometimes enclosed Adena burial mounds, they created increasingly grander ceremonial compounds in the form of marvelously varied and mathematically precise geometrical shapes, plazas, and avenues that sometimes extended for miles.

From their heartland in southern Ohio, the Hopewell, by trade and travel, acquired and exchanged ideas over much of the continent east of the Great Plains. Hopewellian societies, however, did not constitute a political empire, but rather, as Joseph R. Caldwell of the Illinois State Museum once put it, an "interaction sphere"—a dominion of commerce and shared ideas.

The Hopewell practice of mound burial and its attendant ceremonies helped bind together diverse local societies in southern Ohio through common traditions and generated an enormous demand on the part of the elite for ceremonial objects and grave goods—and the exotic materials to make them. This demand could be satisfied only by the establishment of an extraordinary trade network extending from the Rocky Mountains to the Atlantic and from the Great Lakes and Canada to the Gulf Coast.

Ohio Hopewell burial methods did not differ markedly from those adopted by the Adena in their final years. An estimated three-fourths of the burials were cremations; other corpses were laid out in log crypts. Piling up the dirt a basketload at a time around the tombs, workers sometimes unwittingly left their own mark. Henry Shetrone of the Ohio Historical Society wrote of two instances in which he "found individual loads intact, where the weary or careless worker had dropped them on the common heap 'basket and all.' "

What most distinguished these burials from those of the Adena was the astonishing richness of the goods interred with the dead. To provide exhibits for Chicago's World Columbian Exposition of 1893, Warren K. Moorehead excavated 15 of the more than 30 mounds in a 110-acre earthen enclosure near Chillicothe, Ohio, on a farm owned by Cloud Hopewell, which gave the culture its name. Burrowing five trenches into the largest mound—by Moorehead's estimate 500 feet long, 180 feet wide, and 33 feet high—he found a group of 48 burials and an extraordinarily rich assortment of copper wares. Effigies of fish and birds, geometric designs, and a headdress shaped like deer antlers made of copper-covered wood lay together with 23 breastplates and 67 axes, one of which weighed 38 pounds and must have served a ceremonial function only.

Three decades later, Henry Shetrone discovered in the same mound the skeletal remains of a tall young man and a young woman who had been laid side by side. He was much taken with what he saw: "At the head, neck, hips, and knees of the female and completely encircling the skeleton were thousands of pearl beads and buttons of wood and stone covered with copper; extending the full length of the grave along one side was a row of copper ear ornaments; at the wrists of the female were copper bracelets; copper ear ornaments adorned the ears of both, and both wore necklaces of grizzly-bear canines and copper breastplates on the chest." As a final, unexpected touch, affixed to both skeletons were artificial noses made of copper.

Such opulent caches have led some to label the Hopewell the Egyptians of North America. From the original Hopewell group of mounds alone came an estimated 100,000 freshwater pearls. The pearls, taken from mussels in nearby tributaries of the Ohio River, were strung into necklaces or sewn onto clothing. A single grave in another Ohio mound produced 12,000 pearls, 35,000 pearl beads, and 20,000 shell beads as well as a few small sheets of hammered gold and copper, and meteoric iron beads. Other mounds yielded copper figures of birds, turtles, and humans, still more pearls and hundreds of effigy pipes—many of them broken. To Robert Silverberg, a popular writer on the subject, "these gaudy displays of conspicuous consumption" betokened "a flamboyant fondness for excess."

Waterways served as the principal conduits of Hopewell com-

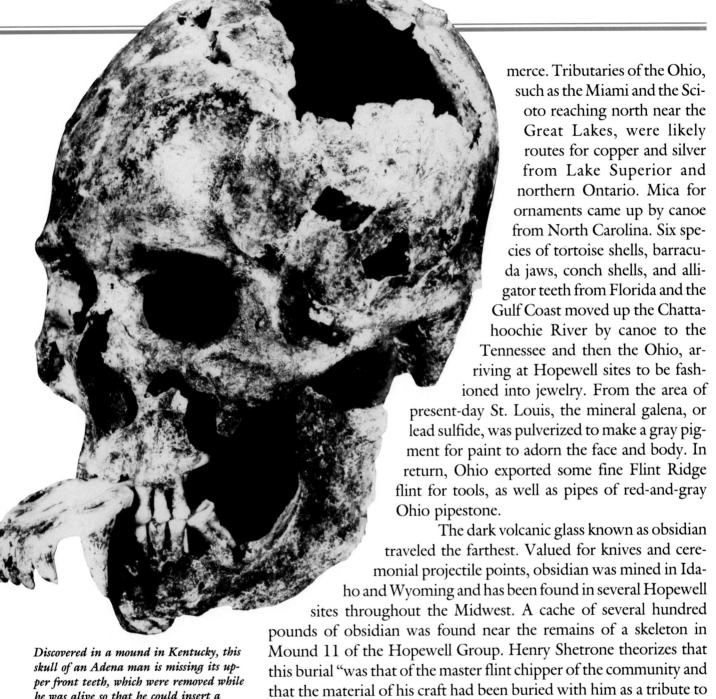

Discovered in a mound in Kentucky, this skull of an Adena man is missing its upper front teeth, which were removed while he was alive so that he could insert a wolf's palate—found beside the skeleton—into his mouth. Probably a shaman, he would have worn it with a wolf mask for ritual or ceremonial functions, perhaps during transformation rites in which he would have assumed a wolflike aspect.

merce. Tributaries of the Ohio, such as the Miami and the Scioto reaching north near the Great Lakes, were likely routes for copper and silver from Lake Superior and northern Ontario. Mica for ornaments came up by canoe from North Carolina. Six species of tortoise shells, barracuda jaws, conch shells, and alligator teeth from Florida and the Gulf Coast moved up the Chattahoochie River by canoe to the Tennessee and then the Ohio, arriving at Hopewell sites to be fashioned into jewelry. From the area of present-day St. Louis, the mineral galena, or lead sulfide, was pulverized to make a gray pigment for paint to adorn the face and body. In return, Ohio exported some fine Flint Ridge flint for tools, as well as pipes of red-and-gray Ohio pipestone.

The dark volcanic glass known as obsidian traveled the farthest. Valued for knives and ceremonial projectile points, obsidian was mined in Idaho and Wyoming and has been found in several Hopewell sites throughout the Midwest. A cache of several hundred pounds of obsidian was found near the remains of a skeleton in Mound 11 of the Hopewell Group. Henry Shetrone theorizes that this burial "was that of the master flint chipper of the community and that the material of his craft had been buried with him as a tribute to his important office."

All these materials as well as the finished products may have changed hands at regional trading points or perhaps even on long-range expeditions carried out by the Hopewell. Artisans transformed the goods pouring in through the trade network into small masterpieces. Lovely shapes from nature were hewn out of mica and copper. Stunningly sculptured stone and clay pipes took animal forms. Some pottery leaped beyond the old utilitarian designs for cooking and

storage to display on its smooth surface birds of prey and other motifs of similar power, incised in the clay and symmetrically repeated.

Human figurines molded from clay or carved from stone and ancient ivory reveal how Hopewell people dressed: Men wore loincloths; women went bare breasted in warm weather, and wore calf-length skirts belted at the waist. One such figurine depicts a man with his hair bunched in a knot on his forehead, the mark of a shaman among later Plains Indians. Another depicts an evident shaman wearing a ceremonial bearskin and holding in his lap a human head. Some show women nursing or carrying babies on their backs.

Both the quality and the quantity of such artifacts seem to point to a class of semiprofessional artisans, not only because of the consummate skill with which they are rendered but also because there are many nearly identical articles—effigy pipes, for example. Though archaeologists have no way of knowing for sure, some of these goods seem to have been made solely for the purpose of interment. Even everyday tools and implements often appear destined for ceremonial burials rather than utilitarian purposes. Or perhaps they were intended as talismans of power for a specific person. In any case, they frequently display no signs of wear. In fact, the eccentric designs of some artifacts—the unusual sizes or shapes of certain copper, mica, and obsidian blades—indicate a preference for aesthetic qualities over actual usefulness.

Archaeologists assume that the special class of artisans and their trade network could have existed only with a sound economic

system and the support of an elite class, which also managed to mobilize and inspire the masses to undertake immense public works projects. The earthen enclosure at Newark, Ohio, once covered more than four square miles of embankments. This interlinking complex of circles, plazas, and avenues—parts of which now are occupied by a public park and a golf course on land owned by the Ohio Historical Society—required almost three million man-hours of labor to move an estimated seven million cubic feet of dirt a basketful at a time over a 300-year timespan.

Just as impressive as the energy employed in earthmoving projects like these was the engineering acumen required to complete them. James A. Marshall, a civil engineer in Illinois who has surveyed and analyzed more than 200 sites, found such precision that he hypothesized the existence of a Hopewell "school of mathematics," which possessed a knowledge of the right triangle and other geometric concepts. According to Marshall, Hopewell engineers, like modern architects, must have first made scale models of their plans and then staked out a formal grid, using a standard unit of measurement of 61.75 yards.

No one knows the significance of the geometric mounds scattered throughout Hopewell territory. Some researchers speculate that in addition to serving as the gathering places of particular clans, each may have represented the symbol of the clan itself. Other investigators find in the Newark complex and in other Hopewell sites not only engineering precision but also exact astronomical align-

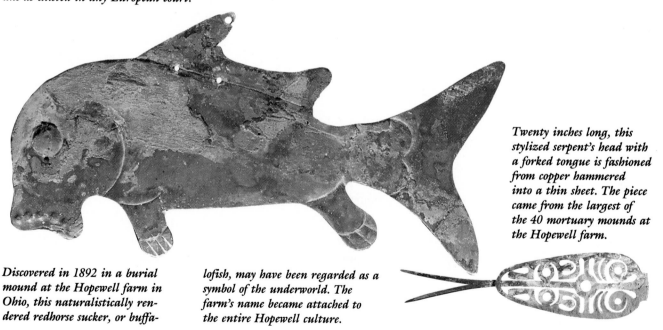

FROM THE BEYOND: BOUNTY OF THE MOUNDS

The Hopewell devoted a variety and quantity of resources to the burial of their dead unsurpassed by any North American culture before or since, placing in their mounds offerings comparable to those found in the tombs of ancient Egypt.

Freshwater pearls—accompanying the dead in abundance—were one of the few items that the Hopewell procured from their own neighborhood. Most other materials they imported from remarkably faraway regions of the continent: copper from the Lake Superior Basin and Ontario, obsidian from Idaho and Wyoming, and exotic shells from the Gulf Coast. The extensive trade networks established by the Hopewell are testimony to both their resourcefulness and the importance they placed on their elaborate grave goods.

Once the raw materials were obtained, highly skilled artisans transformed them into a variety of beautiful and sophisticated pieces—most representing an animal or some other natural object—like those shown here.

Highly prized by the Hopewell, freshwater pearls, like those above, have been found by the hundreds in burials. A scholar claims that "in the age of the Mound Builders there were as many pearls in the possession of a single tribe of Indians as existed in any European court."

Twenty inches long, this stylized serpent's head with a forked tongue is fashioned from copper hammered into a thin sheet. The piece came from the largest of the 40 mortuary mounds at the Hopewell farm.

Discovered in 1892 in a burial mound at the Hopewell farm in Ohio, this naturalistically rendered redhorse sucker, or buffalofish, may have been regarded as a symbol of the underworld. The farm's name became attached to the entire Hopewell culture.

The talon of a bird, cut from fragile sheet mica at least 1,800 years ago, was unearthed miraculously intact from a burial mound at the Hopewell farm. The mica itself probably came from North Carolina.

From the Seip Mound in Ohio, this tortoiseshell trumpeter swan is an example of a continuing motif in North American art. The sawtooth edge is a natural seam between two adjacent pieces of shell on the breastplate of a reptile.

ments, suggesting that the works served as lunar and solar observatories as well as ceremonial centers. However, James B. Griffin, professor emeritus at the University of Michigan and the acknowledged dean of Eastern Woodlands archaeology, warns that concluding "the earthworks were built solely for astronomical observations and with great accuracy is debatable."

The grand ceremonialism of Hopewell society contrasts sharply with the mundane lifestyle of its common people. Until the last three decades or so, archaeologists neglected Hopewell settlements in favor of mound excavations. But during the 1960s, the Ohio archaeologist Olaf Prufer proposed the so-called Hamlet Hypothesis. This notion, based on his own fieldwork and that of others, suggested that Hopewell societies lived in scattered "semipermanent shifting agricultural farmsteads or hamlets" in the general vicinity of vacant ceremonial centers.

Excavations since then have tended to confirm Prufer's idea to some degree. Hopewell people appear to have occupied rectangular or oval houses—not unlike later Indian wigwams—in extended families of up to 13 members. A small number of such households, perhaps only three, constituted the hamlet. Inhabitants from many such hamlets would periodically converge on the ceremonial center for burials or other rituals or to construct new earthworks.

Besides theorizing about settlement patterns, Prufer focused on the longstanding debate about Hopewell subsistence. Did they, like the Adena, depend for food primarily upon hunting small game and harvesting nuts and other wild foods, or did they raise crops, possibly even corn? He looked for an answer as he investigated some three dozen tiny settlement sites in Ohio, none of them much larger than 100 feet in diameter. Then, in 1963, Prufer learned of a possible hamlet—soon to be destroyed by construction of a new highway—in the heart of Hopewell country, two miles south of Chillicothe.

Although surface indications did not look promising, just eight inches down Prufer and his team found a mother lode: a foot-thick deposit of settlement debris of pottery fragments and other artifacts covering an area 95 feet by 140 feet. This rich vein, dating from about AD 400, contained ample evidence of what the hamlet's inhabitants had been eating. Found in the refuse were 2,000 mollusk shells and the remains of wild plants. Prufer also unearthed one individual kernel of corn and two fragmented pieces of an ear, suggesting that the Hopewell had grown the grain early on. This discovery, however, would be disputed by a 1987 follow-up study that showed "historic contamination" of the site by later individuals who may have left the corn there.

Whatever the truth about the Chillicothe site may be, analysis of human bones found in mounds indicates that the Hopewell could have consumed corn only in limited amounts. All the same, Bruce D. Smith of the Smithsonian Institution as well as other researchers insists that, even before the presumed introduction of corn, a crop that would have required regular cultivation, Hopewell people were essentially farmers who placed their settlements in river valleys because of the good soil. Their sites have yielded stone hoes and seed-storage containers that point to an agrarian way of life involving cultivation of at least seven different indigenous plants, including sunflowers and squash.

For all their productive farming and posh ceremonialism, the Hopewell nonetheless went into decline. Between AD 300 and 400—some four centuries after their appearance in southern Ohio—the Hopewellian culture in Ohio faded. Any number of causes have been suggested: disease, famine, civil war, unchecked population growth, the unexplained collapse of trade networks, or climatic change that affected crops and wild foods.

Whatever the cause, by the late 1700s, when the new European masters of the land arrived in force, the earthworks were overgrown, the ceremonial centers lifeless, and only the uncommunicative dead remained. The descendants of the Adena and the Hopewell—those "savage hordes" of pioneer lore—were a demoralized lot, their numbers decimated and their culture in decline from warfare and diseases brought by Europeans. But the achievements of their precursors had been remarkable. The Adena and the Hopewell had managed, as Dr. Griffin points out, to move from the status of hunter-gatherers 10,000 years ago to that of village farmers settled in fairly stable villages and towns. Who knows what they might have accomplished if circumstances had allowed them to develop further along a uniquely Indian path.

STUPENDOUS PILES OF EARTH

Newcomers to the Midwest in the early part of the 19th century did not have to go far to see massive earthworks of mysterious origin. "There is hardly a rising town, or a farm of an eligible situation, in whose vicinity some of these remains may not be found," wrote one such traveler in 1811. Indeed, St. Louis was known as Mound City, so numerous were the man-made hillocks dotting the site at the time.

Back east, public curiosity about these monuments would be fed by a hyperbolic press. A May 1883 issue of a New York tabloid, *Frank Leslie's Illustrated Newspaper,* described and showed the Menard Mound *(above),* an impossibly proportioned "huge pillar" in Desha County, Arkansas, that was said to rise 100 feet; in actuality, it was 35 feet high. The paper had no need to exaggerate; there were plenty of bigger earthworks with which to impress its readers. The largest of the pyramid-like mounds at the eight-square-mile Indian city of Cahokia, Illinois, for example, rivaled Egypt's Great Pyramid, with a base covering more than 16 acres. "What a stupendous pile of earth!" commented the 1811 traveler. "To heap up such a mass must have required years, and the labor of thousands."

Fortunately, serious students of the mounds—the work, it turned out, of prehistoric societies, the Adena, the Hopewell, and the Mississippians—made drawings and surveys of many of the sites. "No exertion was spared to ensure entire accuracy," proudly wrote Ephraim Squier and Edwin Davis, authors of an 1848 report on earthworks in the Mississippi Valley. Most of the monuments these and other researchers examined are gone today, plowed under by farmers and urban developers, paved over by highways, and plundered by looters. But the records serve to summon up this vanished heritage. Contemporary archaeologists use them to study the once-widespread monuments and determine their purposes, as well as to obtain insights into the masterful builders themselves.

One of the largest existing Adena mounds, Miamisburg Mound in western Ohio, shown at left in a recent photograph, measured at least 68 feet high before excavators skimmed off part of the top in 1869. An 1848 engraving (below) shows that the earthwork has changed little. An Adena mound in Marietta, Ohio, seen in the background engraving, is another of the few to have escaped destruction; it became a settlers' graveyard.

EARTHWORKS: A PURPOSEFUL LABOR

Across the Ohio Valley, the Adena and the Hopewell reshaped the horizon with thousands of earthen mounds, all built with one major purpose in mind—honoring their dead. Virtual cemeteries, the cone-shaped creations of the Adena housed 50 bodies or more—and reached anywhere from a few yards to more than 80 feet in height.

Earthworks constructed by the Hopewell served as mass graves as well, but these people placed their dead closer to the surface and expanded the mounds horizontally rather than upward, giving them a variety of shapes. Also unlike the Adena, the Hopewell lavished their dead with magnificent troves of grave goods that would later make the burial mounds prime targets for treasure hunters.

In the Mississippi Valley and on the Gulf Coast, a separate tradition flourished some 600 years after the decline of the Hopewell societies. These later tribes constructed earthen monuments of their own, but for an altogether different purpose. Rather than functioning as resting places for the dead, the mounds—often immense and flat-topped—served primarily as centers of public life and as foundations for important buildings that emphasized the power of the elite.

Monks Mound at Cahokia, Illinois (above), rises to a height of nearly a hundred feet, making it the largest man-made earthen mound north of Mexico. "We would scarcely believe it to be the work of human hands," wrote archaeologist William McAdams, who published an engraving of the Mississippian work in 1887 (right). He complained, however, that "the view is so much foreshortened that it gives no correct idea of the size of the monument." The house on the highest of the four terraces was built by a man who hoped to live "above the malaria" that infected the region.

This 1894 drawing from a work by Cyrus Thomas, appointed by the Smithsonian's Bureau of Ethnology to investigate the origins of mounds, shows an interior view of a Hopewell mound in Dunleith, Illinois, labeled number 16. Thomas accurately portrayed the shallow hill of earth and the log crypt beneath, used only for the elite, but the posture of the skeletons is fanciful—the Hopewell never buried their dead sitting up.

A drawing from Thomas's book shows a box grave, a type often seen among southern Illinois Mississippian graves. These sites did not become mounds, nor were pits normally used by other Mississippians for the dead. As befitted their status, however, rulers often were interred beneath the floors of mound temples.

The round charnel house pictured here—based on a reconstruction by modern Adena scholar Don Dragoo—sheltered burial preparations, the displayed body, and new or open graves. At some point, the Adena would burn such huts with the remains and heap soil over the ashes, forming a new mound. The cross section (right) shows distinct layers—reflecting varying soil composition and vegetation—as new burials took place. Group of Sepulchral Mounds (background), from Squier and Davis's book, shows that burial mounds were often clustered.

RESTING PLACES FOR THE NOBLE DEAD

Dating from around 500 BC, the earliest Adena mounds began with the interment of single bodies. Relatives would lay out the corpse or skeletal remains in a shallow pit lined and covered with bark, and then fashion a hump of earth above it. Over time—often the passage of several generations—kinsmen continued to bring their dead to the site, sprinkling the remains with powdered red ocher and adding a few personal objects for accompaniment in the beyond. As new mourners put others to rest and tamped down each successive layer of earth, the mound grew to an impressive size. Later in their history, the Adena created log tombs as well as bark-lined graves and devised even more elaborate crypts constructed inside burial, or charnel, houses on the mound site *(below)*.

The Hopewell, too, used the charnel house—preparing, cremating, and burying their dead in shallow graves or log vaults within its walls. When space ran out, they dismantled or burned the house and covered the area with a mound of earth. Unlike the Adena, they interred their dead with numerous funerary goods.

CIRCLES OF REVERENCE

In 1848 Ephraim Squier and Edwin Davis came to the "irresistible" conclusion that the earthen walls wrapped fortresslike around many Adena and Hopewell mounds were held "sacred, and thus set apart as 'tabooed' or consecrated ground" by their creators. Although some 19th-century thinkers, especially military men, thought that the walls were fortifications, archaeologists today agree with Squier and Davis that the rings marked literally hallowed ground.

The late Adena built simple enclosures consisting of circular walls and ditches up to 200 feet in diameter, interrupted by a single gateway, that encompassed a moatlike ditch and a central mound, much like the system shown in the Squier and Davis illustration *Circle and* *Mound, Greenup County, Kentucky (background)*. In addition to monuments like these, the Hopewell built enclosures that were far more elaborate and imaginative than those of the Adena, making use of various geometric configurations. Often the enclosures clustered in systems that stretched across the landscape for miles and contained dozens of mounds.

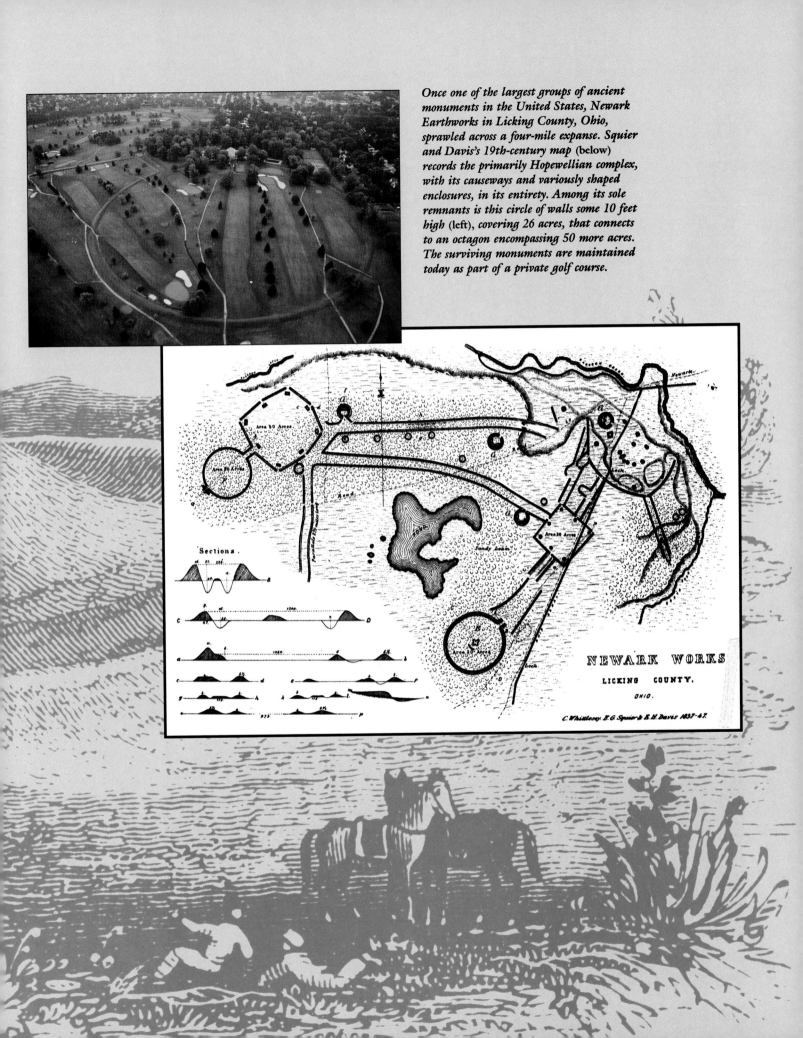

Once one of the largest groups of ancient monuments in the United States, Newark Earthworks in Licking County, Ohio, sprawled across a four-mile expanse. Squier and Davis's 19th-century map (below) records the primarily Hopewellian complex, with its causeways and variously shaped enclosures, in its entirety. Among its sole remnants is this circle of walls some 10 feet high (left), covering 26 acres, that connects to an octagon encompassing 50 more acres. The surviving monuments are maintained today as part of a private golf course.

Sections.

NEWARK WORKS
LICKING COUNTY.
OHIO.
C. Whittlesey, E.G. Squier & E.H. Davis 1837-47.

Second only to Cahokia in size, the earth-works at Moundville, Alabama, formed the hub of a Mississippian region that may have had as many as 10,000 people. Its 20 large platform mounds—dating from between AD 1250 and 1500—covered more than 300 fertile acres (below). The 1905 map at left shows the distribution, shapes, and relative sizes of all of the mounds, which were clustered together at a bend in the Black Warrior River.

MOUNDS NEAR MOUNDVILLE, ALA.
Scale in feet
1905

BLACK WARRIOR RIVER

AMERICA'S OWN PYRAMIDS

"There are many pyramids in the United States, regular, perfect pyramids of earth, and not faced with stone," marveled William McAdams, who like many others noted a startling resemblance between the immense mounds of the Mississippians and the great monuments of Egypt and Mexico.

Usually constructed with rectangular bases, the largest mounds dwarfed those of the Adena and Hopewell cultures; Monks Mound, the massive formation at Cahokia, contained some 22 million cubic feet of earth. Built to elevate temples, public buildings, and noble residences above the common ground, Mississippian mounds were of necessity flat-topped and often boasted two or three terraces, as is illustrated by a 19th-century drawing of the De Soto Mound in Arkansas *(background)*, named for the Spanish conquistador, who is said to have camped there. These earthworks were the hallmark of ceremonial centers shared by small, independent communities located as much as 10 to 20 miles away.

TEMPLE MOUND BUILDERS: THE HIGH AND THE MIGHTY

Forrest E. Clements, head of the Department of Anthropology at the University of Oklahoma, never quite got over the "shock and grief" he felt in the fall of 1935 when he discovered what had happened to one of the United States' greatest Indian sites. Writing about the experience 10 years later, he described how "the great mound had been tunneled through and through, gutted in a frenzy of haste. Sections of cedar poles lay scattered on the ground, fragments of feather and fur textiles littered the whole area; it was impossible to take a single step without scuffing up broken pieces of pottery, sections of engraved shell, and beads of shell, stone, and bone. The site was abandoned; the diggers had completed their work."

The 33-foot-tall mound—actually the largest of a group of nine—lay near the small town of Spiro, Oklahoma. It consisted of four conjoined humps, resembling a sea serpent in profile. Occasional minor pitting by unauthorized amateurs had revealed that the earthwork was, in fact, a burial mound containing promising quantities of grave goods. The destruction Clements confronted, however, was the work not of weekend pot hunters but of a band of commercial scavengers who happened to have a legal lease on the property and who regarded its exploitation as a way of turning a fast buck during some of the worst days of the Great Depression.

Its gaping mouth and narrow, lifeless eyes suggest to some scholars that this ceramic vessel from an Arkansan mound represents a member of its society's honored dead. Mississippian cultures were known to venerate the remains of their most revered citizens.

Picking his way through the devastation, Clements saw three tunnels driven into the heart of the cone from different directions, all meeting in a large, irregularly shaped chamber some 15 to 20 feet across and about eight feet high. Rumor had it that the floor of the vault had been strewn with hammered copper breastplates, ornamental ear spools, pottery vessels, effigy pipes, and engraved conch shells. At one end of the vault an altar had reputedly supported a large urn full of pearls; and near the altar lay a single shrouded skeleton.

Now, Clements found only heaps of loose dirt, gin bottles, and cigarette butts on the uneven floor. When he studied the walls he saw no trace of alleged ancient tapestries, only the gouges left by recent excavation. It seemed that the vandalism had been complete. He was both appalled and puzzled.

The mounds had for many years been regarded with a decent and distant respect by locals who recognized them as ancient burial sites and would by no means have disturbed them. Some said that their mules shied as they passed these piles of earth, and that strange fires flickered atop them on dark nights. One woman who lived close by, known as Aunt Rachel Brown, told neighbors about waking up in the middle of the night to see shimmering sheets of blue flame hanging over the large conical mound, illuminating a most extraordinary scene: a team of cats, harnessed in tandem, pulling a small wagon around and around the summit.

Not the most terrifying of haunts, certainly, but the mounds' out-of-the-way location kept curio seekers pretty much at bay—that is, until 1933, when a group of six local men formed the Pocala Mining Company and obtained a two-year lease on the site from a new owner of the land less reverent than Rachel Brown. Almost immediately the so-called miners began hauling out spectacular artifacts, which they sold at the site and through the mail to the antiquities market. These activities came to the attention of the National Research Council Committee on State Archaeological Surveys, which asked Clements to keep an eye on the excavations. With map in hand he tracked down the place where the locals said "the fellows were mining the old mound."

For the better part of two years, as an employee of the University of Oklahoma, Clements watched over the lessees and made every effort to keep them digging slowly and cautiously by invoking the profit motive—unbroken artifacts, he pointed out, fetched higher prices. Unfortunately, university funds ran out in the summer of

Complete with sensational headline, a feature story in the December 15, 1935, Kansas City Star *makes much of recent discoveries at the Spiro Mound in Oklahoma. The finds were indeed archaeological treasures, but the haphazard digging—conducted by commercial pot hunters—destroyed as much evidence as it produced. Several months after the article appeared, the University of Oklahoma and the Oklahoma Historical Society obtained a lease to the site, and systematic investigations began. The photo above shows society founder W. P. Campbell displaying some of the artifacts recovered.*

1935, and Clements accepted a temporary job in California to tide him over until fall.

That last summer was a bonanza for the diggers. With Clements gone, they threw caution to the winds and blasted into the mound with dynamite. Trundling ceremonial and decorative objects out by the wheelbarrow-load, the entrepreneurs brought into the 20th century some of the finest relics of pre-Columbian America.

And the 20th century was waiting: Dealers and collectors stood by with cash in hand to haggle over the exquisite conch-shell cups and pendants engraved with mystical motifs, the outsize axes and maces, the copper plaques and human-effigy tobacco pipes, the carved wooden masks and human figurines, the glistening ornamental beads. Surviving account books show records of transactions involving "shell beads—1,200 lbs." and "pearl beads—2 gallons."

This phenomenal inventory of plunder from Spiro was but a small portion of the tangible legacy bequeathed to modern America by a prehistoric people who flourished between AD 800 and 1500.

Spanning half the continent, their realm reached from Wisconsin all the way to the Gulf of Mexico and from the Georgia coast westward through Tennessee, Ohio, Illinois, Arkansas, and Texas to Oklahoma. Where they originated, however, no one yet knows. Scholars use the term "Mississippian Tradition" when they talk about them since many of the mound centers are located in the Mississippi Valley.

What is perhaps most amazing about the Mississippians is how quickly their culture spread throughout the American heartland, achieving the highest level of endemic development in the New World north of Mexico. Their rise had largely to do with the introduction of a new and convenient food source from Mesoamerica—improved strains of corn that allowed Mississippian communities to make the leap from the mere subsistence farming of the Adena and the Hopewell to a more luxurious way of life. And as the standard of living went up, skilled craftsmen—both men and women—were called upon by the elite to turn out fine ornaments and tools like those dug from the Spiro mound, treasures their owners fully expected to take to the grave with them.

There was much to stimulate and inspire the Mississippians. Many if not all of their far-flung settlements participated in an extensive trade network facilitated by the rivers, creeks, and streams on or near which they lived. Out of such contact with others came the exchange of ideas as well as goods, helping to forge common bonds—and instilling common beliefs.

Central to the Mississippians' religious practice were their flat-topped pyramids, so ubiquitous in their society that the people are often referred to as the Temple Mound Builders. These finely engineered, handmade hillocks usually ranged in height from 18 to 60 feet, with temples, council buildings, and residences for the elite perched on the summits. Some were built close together and served essentially as ceremonial centers, as perhaps Spiro might have been. Atop them elaborate rituals that involved a belief in an upper and a lower world may have been conducted, drawing participants from all over the local region and helping confer on them a common identity. But many of the centers also functioned as towns, with the houses of the common folk ranged around the massive earthworks.

Since the Temple Mound Builders left no written record and died out centuries ago, how can a picture of this majestic American culture be pieced together? In fact, early European visitors saw surviving vestiges of the Mississippians' society and set down their

A RESPECT FOR THE DEAD

In 1927 Dr. Don F. Dickson, a practicing chiropractor and avocational archaeologist, began excavating under the apple orchard on his family's farm in Fulton County, Illinois. What he uncovered there would become the subject of a bitter controversy between Native Americans and local residents.

Dickson Mounds, as the entire 162-acre site is now known, includes remnants of prehistoric villages, camps, and fortified towns in the Illinois River valley. Specifically, the name refers to a small group of mounds excavated by Dr. Dickson and studied by archaeologists from around the country. The mounds include the remains of 251 Mississippians who settled in the region around AD 1100. Left as found, the skeletons were put on display in a state-funded museum built to protect the site, along with the pots, tools, and other objects uncovered in the vicinity. It was around this exhibit that the maelstrom of controversy was to revolve.

In the early 1970s, Indians in Illinois and elsewhere began agitating to have the human remains reburied, out of respect for the spirits of the dead. Residents of the area, which is noteworthy for its more than 3,000 prehistoric archaeological sites, felt differently, arguing that the exhibit had been presented tastefully and that it accurately reflected the tradition and history of the region.

Whether museums should display or store Native American remains and sacred objects has been debated for years. Reacting to pressure from Indian advocacy groups, large institutions such as the Smithsonian and Chicago's Field Museum began returning human remains and other items to tribes that could demonstrate some cultural or biological connection to them. And in 1990, Congress passed the Native American Graves Protection and Repatriation Act requiring federal agencies and museums receiving federal funding to determine the cultural affiliations of their Indian skeletal collections and to notify possible present-day descendants.

Though the Dickson Mounds Museum does not fall under the purview of the federal law, the state of Illinois cooperates with historic tribes in identifying human remains. But living descendants of the Mississippians, who left the valley around AD 1350, cannot be traced. To the Native Americans objecting to the display, however, this was immaterial. And on April 6, 1991, they decided to take matters into their own hands. Jumping over a railing enclosing the dimly lit exhibit, activists symbolically shoveled dirt onto several of the exposed graves.

The protest helped galvanize the governor and the state legislature into taking action on the issue. On April 3, 1992, the state of Illinois ordered the museum's Native American burial exhibit—the last of its kind in the United States—to shut down.

impressions; these, in turn, have been supported by subsequent archaeological findings. Taken together, the objects and the early accounts have provided enough details and clues to rescue the Mississippians from obscurity and give them their due place in history.

Slashing through the American Southeast in the mid-16th century, the Spanish explorer Hernando de Soto's band of treasure hunters could not help noticing that many river-valley communities were dominated by most unusual earthworks: huge, flat-topped, rectangular mounds rising 50 feet and more. As they learned from the Indian inhabitants, the chief's dwelling stood on one high mound and the village temple on another. Mildly curious, de Soto and his men paused to watch the enlargement of some of the bigger specimens, already so high and steep that the workers had built ramps to bring dirt to the summit. Basketfuls at a time, they dumped it on the surface and stamped down vigorously until it was firm and flat. From the top, the Spaniards could look down upon an open plaza. Beyond lay the great forest canopy, with here and there a break to reveal a flood-plain landscape of cypress swamps and oxbow lakes.

But sightseeing lulls were rare for de Soto's men, who, like their leader, may have been jaded by what they had seen of splendor in Central and South America. Besides, they had little respect for the "heathens" in their path. In an obstinate quest for gold, they burned villages and massacred inhabitants on their meandering route through 10 southern states. In addition to the rampant, outright killing, the Europeans left a pernicious legacy of disease that would decimate indigenous tribes long after their departure.

The Spaniards' superior technology—and their horses—gave them an insurmountable edge against their foes; but if they expected the Indians to capitulate meekly or run away, they were sorely mistaken. Expedition members recorded that any conquistador who foolishly strayed from camp was shot from ambush and immediately scalped or beheaded. De Soto's men soon discovered to their dismay that chain-mail armor provided inadequate protection against Indian projectiles. During the night, Indians would disinter Spanish burials, hack the bodies to pieces, and hang them from trees as a morbid reminder to the living.

The local tribes exhibited fierce tenacity in their resistance all along the interlopers' line of march. Women and even small children would fight to the death, or kill themselves, to avoid capture. It was a grisly campaign that produced no winners. The Spaniards who survived the grueling trek—de Soto not among them—went home empty-handed. The native population was decimated, and its culture fell into decline. But in their response to foreign invasion, these Mound Builders clearly displayed the mettle that had previously raised the Mississippian culture to its apex.

Later, toward the very end of its millenium-long tenure, surviving pockets of the old way of life provided another window on history, played out to European visitors more interested than de Soto in recording details of what they saw. The Natchez, for example, were a tightly structured tribe living in several settlements near the present-day city of Natchez, Mississippi. They had clung the longest to mound-building tradition and the complex, colorful culture it represented in its prime. Adulterated perhaps, decaying, and seen through foreign eyes with preconceived notions, their society was nonetheless a living holdover from the past. Antoine Le Page du Pratz, a Dutch settler in the Louisiana Colony in the early 1700s, lived for eight years among the Natchez, becoming their preeminent diarist. To him and through him, as to no previous inquirer, the Temple Mound Builders revealed themselves in all their splendor.

The supreme ruler of the Natchez, du Pratz learned, was the Great Sun, a living deity believed to be a direct descendant or even the actual brother of the sun itself. He was assisted by a supreme war chief, his own earthly brother Tattooed Serpent, and a number of other immediate Sun family members including Women Suns—his mother and sisters. Beneath them in the administrative hierarchy were the chiefs of the seven individual districts, or satellite villages. These men and other high officials were lesser relatives of the Great Sun, and highly respected as members of the first family. A notch lower on the scale were the Nobles, then the Honored Men; and, much lower, the commoners, who did the less-than-glorious work of procuring food for their masters and hauling baskets of soil to top off the mounds. These wretches, according to the Europeans, were known by the Natchez language equivalent of Stinkers, or Stinkards.

The Great Sun himself lived atop a platform mound in the tribe's administrative and religious capital, described by some observers as the Grand Village, although it was no larger than the rest. Beyond the capital were the other settlements. Each had its own political and religious hub, consisting of a temple mound and several mound-based dwelling places for the elite, with a central plaza completing the layout. The rest of the community was scattered throughout the district in the form of isolated households and hamlets where people farmed small patches of land. Everything about the Great Sun was impressive, not just his dwelling place atop his massive mound. He wore a regal crown of white feathers, and his feet never touched bare ground. Mats were spread before him when he walked, which was seldom; for the most part he was carried around on a flower-canopied litter of a type whose remains have been uncovered by archaeologists at various Mississippian burial sites. Although, as du Pratz observed, he commanded the total submission of his people, the Great Sun recognized that his jurisdiction was dwindling. "Our nation," he said, "was formerly very numerous and very powerful; it extended more than 12 days' journey from east to west, and more than 15 from south to north." Now it had shrunk to a scattering of small communities housing probably fewer than 4,000 people. Or so he claimed; this was still a large figure, almost certainly inflated.

Still, the Great Sun's power over his subjects' lives and property continued to be absolute. As another observer, the French Jesuit historian Pierre Charlevoix, noted, "The fathers of families never fail to bring to the temple the first fruits of everything they gather; and they do the same by all the presents that are made to the nation. They expose them at the door of the temple, the keeper of which after having presented them to the spirits carries them to the great chief, who distributes them to whom he pleases."

Yet Great Suns, like mortals, died. And when a Great Sun departed this world, as the French observed, his successor would come not from his or his brothers' line, but from that of his closest female relative. Succession was matrilineal and Sun mothers were respected, but only men could rule. Across the open plaza from the Great Sun's highly placed dwelling reared another great mound, a daily reminder of the journey through death into eternal life. Wide steps led up one side to reach the wooden temple built upon the earthwork's level summit. Inside the temple, the skeletal remains of the previous Great Sun lay upon a funerary litter; nearby, an eternal fire burned. In his time, this high chief had been laid to rest with the great and awful ceremony accorded all Suns.

In 1725, du Pratz and a number of French colleagues were privileged and horrified to witness the burial rites of the war chief Tattooed Serpent, brother of the Great Sun. As was customary, the dead warrior's entire entourage accompanied him, more or less voluntarily, in death: two wives, a sister—who reportedly went with some reluctance—his military aide, head servant, doctor, nurse, pipe bearer, the man who made his war clubs, and assorted other retainers. In addition, there were volunteers who offered themselves or their children as additional companions, thinking to gain favor for themselves in life or in death.

When the body of Tattooed Serpent had lain in state for the allotted time, elaborately clothed and painted and wearing moccasins for his journey, his fellow travelers were escorted to death mats outside the temple. With deerskins placed over their heads, they were strangled with cords. Not an attractive prospect for even the most enthusiastic volunteer, but wives above all were willing to face it. They were convinced of an other-world life far better than the earthly life they knew. Tattooed Serpent's favorite wife, shortly before the end, tried to explain to du Pratz and his company that they should not mourn the war chief or his family and friends: "What does it matter? He is in the country of the spirits, and in two days I will go to join him and will tell him that I have seen your hearts shake at the sight of his dead body. Do not grieve. We will be friends for a much longer time in the country of the spirits than in this, because one does not die there again. It is always fine weather, one is never hungry, and men do not make war there any more."

After the ceremony, Tattooed Serpent's house was burned to its foundations. In time, if custom held, the mound would be raised to cover the blackened residue and a new structure would be built. But custom did not hold. The Natchez were a reduced and weakened people as a result of the spread of deadly smallpox and influenza germs brought in from the Old World. When their fragile friendship with the French erupted into open warfare in 1729, the Natchez managed only one final gasp of rebellion before being virtually annihilated. With them, the last life signs of Mississippian culture were snuffed out.

In other portions of their erstwhile realm, the Mound Builders and their imposing monuments would lie hidden and forgotten. Slowly, eerily, the past began to reemerge. In the mid-1730s, a colonist in Georgia observed a topo-

Just a little over five inches tall, this figurine unearthed near Cahokia may represent a woman at work: She appears to be kneeling on ears of corn before a metate, a stone tablet on which corn was ground. Her long, straight hair is pulled back behind her ears, and she is wearing a short wraparound skirt.

graphical oddity at Ocmulgee, east of Macon, and made note (incorrectly, as was later learned) of "three Mounts raised by the Indians over three of their Great Kings who were killed in the Wars." In the years to come, wayfarers would pause to contemplate the origin of these abandoned works, only to learn that the local tribes had no traditions regarding the mounds or their builders. However, ghostly singing—they were told—could sometimes be heard at the mound sites in the hours before dawn.

A little over a hundred miles northwest of Ocmulgee and its haunting voices was a mound complex called Etowah, described in 1819 for the readers of *Silliman's Journal,* a popular science magazine of the day, by the Reverend Elias Cornelius. Noting that he had seen many artificial mounds in his time and read of many more, he added that he had never before seen one "of such dimension as that which I am now to describe." Accompanied to the site by eight Indian chiefs, Cornelius noticed a pit some 20 feet wide and 10 feet deep. To his surprise, there was no piled-up dirt on either side of it. "But I did not long doubt to what place the earth had been removed," he wrote, "for I had scarcely proceeded 200 yards when, through the thick forest trees, a stupendous pile met the eye, whose dimensions were in full proportion to the intrenchment."

Seeking to gauge its proportions, Cornelius cut a long vine and did the best he could. "The perpendicular height cannot be less than 75 feet," he guessed with the aid of his improvised tape measure. "The circumference of the base, including the feet of three parapets, measured 1,114 feet." The summit was a flat platform so deeply engulfed in the luxuriant growth of perhaps 200 years that he could not examine it as well as he wished. "One beech tree near the top," he noted, "measured 10 feet 9 inches in circumference."

Cornelius was struck by the chiefs' reaction to such mounds. "On these great works of art the Indians gazed with as much curiosity as any white man," he observed. "I inquired of the oldest chief if the natives had any tradition respecting them, to which he answered in the negative. I then requested each to say what he supposed was their origin. Neither could tell, though they all agreed in saying, 'They were never put up by our people.'" What must also have amazed such early investigators as Cornelius was the distribution of these extraordinary mounds over a wide portion of the United States.

Although they shared many similarities, the far-flung settlements differed in their size, grandeur, and local culture. Some were

modest places, some immense. The most spectacular of them all was at Cahokia, Illinois, in what is known as the American Bottom—that abundant agricultural area where the Missouri River disgorges into the Mississippi. In its prime, Cahokia measured some five and a half square miles and may have had up to 12,000 residents. By all estimates and speculations, it was the largest and most populous settlement in prehistoric North America—as big, certainly, as many European cities of the day.

Members of archaeologist A. R. Kelly's crew excavate the floor of the Earthlodge, a circular council house discovered at Ocmulgee in 1934. In an early paper he wrote on the dig, Kelly noted that the mound had first been explored because it appeared to be "something more than one of 'the red hills of Georgia.'"

From his readings and observations during the late 1800s, Cyrus Thomas, head of the Smithsonian's Division of Mound Exploration, correctly deduced that the man-made plateaus were the elevated foundations of important structures. It was he who first called their creators the Temple Mound Builders because they did indeed build temple mounds as distinct from the mortuary mounds of the

Adena and the Hopewell. However, he did not intend to imply that all the structures supported temples. Nonetheless, the name stuck.

The essential distinguishing characteristic of the mounds, however, was not their imposing size or even their unique shape. It was, as with all real estate, their location. Widespread as they were, the tribal groups sharing the Mississippian Tradition also shared the same general habitat: the flood plains of the Mississippi Valley and the rich alluvial bottoms of other eastern rivers, a natural larder.

Oddly enough, although Thomas and his fellow 19th-century archaeologists devoted much time and effort to the study of Georgian mounds, they somehow bypassed the elevations at Ocmulgee. Not until the end of 1933 did the Smithsonian's Bureau of American Ethnology—largely underwritten by the New Deal's Works Progress Administration—undertake excavations at the site of the Mounts of Great Kings, first observed in the 1730s.

Gradually, methodically, the noted archaeologist A. R. Kelly and his team unzipped the covers of time and unearthed an occupancy going back well beyond the Temple Mound Builders themselves—to about 3000 BC—and ending

Sliced clean through to make way for a railroad line, Ocmulgee's vast burial mound reveals the distinct layers of a succession of constructions in this photograph taken in 1934. To ensure an accurate recording of the layers' varying colors, the meticulous Kelly also commissioned an artist to paint the scene.

around AD 1200, when the mound-building tenants abandoned Ocmulgee for reasons unknown. Over the course of eight years the team patiently shifted tons of dirt from one pile to another, uncovering hundreds of thousands of objects—human bones, arrow points, tools, pots, and pottery shards.

In the dry tones of a man writing "A Preliminary Report on Archaeological Explorations at Macon, Georgia," Kelly declared that the first temple mounds at Ocmulgee took shape around AD 900. He conjured up a picture of a community that lived off the bounty of the land with such success that they were able to establish a settlement that was, as his diggings revealed, no mere village but rather a major ceremonial center.

On high ground safe from rising river waters, they had erected a township of thatched houses and rectangular wooden temples, some for summer use and some for winter. A great temple mound, nearly 50 feet high and about 300 feet wide, towered over lesser examples that lay around it. Almost as eye-catching was a burial mound of unusual shape and in rather pitiful condition. It had been partly destroyed by steam-shovel excavations to provide flat ground on which to lay tracks of the Central of Georgia Railway.

Kelly's crew made a neater vertical crosscut and found that the mound consisted of five distinct layers of mixed sand and clay, one piled on top of the other. Not merely layers, each constituted a mound in itself. Deep within the structure, in the foundation of the innermost mound, lay the entombed remains of six villagers. Each body was liberally bedecked with beads of shell and other simple adornments. Anyone hoping to find gold, silver, or precious gems would have been crushingly disappointed. A wide clay stairway led to the summit of the first mound. Above lay four more compacted layers of clay, each of which—judging by the remnants of posts that Kelly found—had supported a wooden building.

The temple mounds showed much the same kind of layering. Apparently, the earliest temple at any given locale sat at ground level. When it was razed, a new platform of clay over the ruins served as a foundation for the next. But what was their purpose?

There were still no definitive answers, but there were clues. Kelly's team believed the temples to have been gathering places for council meetings and communal rituals. In one partly intact temple

Each hewn from a single piece of stone, then ground and polished, these foot-long axes show no signs of ordinary wear and were doubtless never used as tools or weapons. They were probably displayed by their owners as symbols of rank or office.

they found a clear circular area, 42 feet in diameter, bounded by a clay wall. A low-slung, circular clay bench near the wall's base could have accommodated 47 persons sitting side by side. Whoever they were, these nameless, faceless beings—almost certainly all male—encircled an area containing a central firepit and a clay platform in the shape of an eagle. Such effigies of birds of prey became a common symbol throughout the Southeast during late Temple Mound days.

Why did the Mississippians build these mounds so high? Some leading authorities on their culture point out that in many societies the world over, elevation equals power. During this same time period, feudal barons in Europe situated their castles on lofty crags looking down over their serfs. So, too, Mississippian leaders raised man-made hills in the generally flat surroundings to place themselves above the commoners and closer to the Upper World. The mounds served the elite as a clearly defined claim on the land, while emphasizing their ties to the past and their ancestors and defining the center of their society and their universe.

But then, as mysteriously as they had come into existence, the Mound Builders of Ocmulgee disappeared. The fires went out, the ceremonies stopped, and the hubbub of daily life ceased. At some time around AD 1200—long before the Spanish-initiated holocaust—people stopped living here. If they were wiped out by plague or fire or war, there is no sign of it; if they simply left, abandoning the place, there is no apparent reason. Only overgrown mounds remained, a curiosity for passing travelers and a neglected monument to the human beings whose Promethean labors had built them. No wonder their spirits wailed in the darkness before dawn.

What were the Mississippians like? In trying to paint a picture of vanished peoples, archaeologists often look for evidence of what they ate, since the relative ease or difficulty in procuring the neces-

Of unknown significance, these ear ornaments carved from seashells were relatively common in Mississippian cultures from approximately AD 1000 to 1300, dropping out of use thereafter. Some versions were made of copper, but nearly all bear the same haunting features.

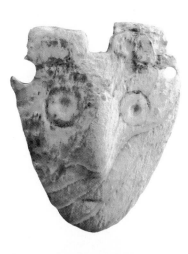

sities of life bears directly on the amount of time and energy that can be devoted to other pursuits.

Hard evidence for the Mississippian diet is limited to the rich terrain itself, and to the fragmentary remains of plants and animal bones turned up by excavations at site after site—a deer mandible here, a hoard of desiccated berries or a pile of nutshells there. The same plants and animals are identifiable throughout the river-valley flood plains of eastern portions of the country. There may have been variations from time to time and place to place that have not yet been revealed. But it would seem that, on the whole, the Temple Mound Builders' menu was a rich and varied one.

As hunter-gatherers, they needed do little more than reach out and grab the well-balanced food stocks of the land and its waters—ample quantities of fish, water-fowl, white-tailed deer, turkey, raccoon, opossum, rabbit, and squirrel; nuts, fruits, berries, wild herbs, and seeds in great variety. They also tilled the fertile flood-plain soils, which made excellent fields to grow corn, squash, and beans, along with minor crops such as sunflowers and chenopod, a plant of the goosefoot family related to beets and spinach. It would be a nice scene: a Mississippian dinner table—or its equivalent—heaped with the catch of the season, perhaps turkey or deer or catfish, accompanied by a variety of vegetables, and attended by a little family group.

From what archaeologists, anthropologists, and historians have gleaned about southeastern Indians—pre-Columbian and historic—it is likely that the Mississippian mound-building societies regarded men and women as virtually two different species. If this scenario is correct, men would have gone to war, provided meat by hunting and fishing, cleared ground for building, and taken part in

This remarkably well preserved cedar mask from Spiro, Oklahoma, combines human features with deer antlers; shell inlays represent the eyes and mouth. Wooden objects rarely survived the damp climate of the East, but conditions at Spiro yielded a number of such relics.

male-only gatherings in private chambers or meeting grounds in the plaza. Women would have gathered wild foods, cultivated crops, worked around the homestead, and socialized with one another during the day. It is likely, too, that the men had it easier, talking politics and playing ball, while their mothers, wives, and sisters hauled firewood, cooked, made everyday pots and baskets and clothing.

A tip-off to woman's role in Mound Builder society may be discerned in the mass of ornamental artifacts that surfaced during explorations of the better-known temple mound sites, such as those at Spiro; Etowah, Georgia; and Moundville, Alabama. Magnificent small pieces of artistry in wood, clay, shell, stone, and hammered copper came to light: ax- and macelike tools, finely detailed in design and highly polished, masks in the shape of animal heads or men with curiously inhuman features, stone disks, clay bowls, and shell cups bearing a broad range of compelling designs. Effigies and effigy pipes depict men sitting, crouching, kneeling, bending over fallen enemies. In contrast appears the figure of a woman—grinding corn.

Other female figurines are occasionally unearthed, sometimes with the woman paired with a man, but this is the exception rather than the rule. Two fine ceremonially interred pieces, found near Cahokia, portray single subjects. Both are thought to be fertility icons. One depicts a woman kneeling on ears of corn, suggesting not only the mutual fertility of the woman and the soil but also her primary occupation; the other, a kneeling figure as well, digs with a short-handled hoe into the back of a serpent whose body is sprouting gourd-bearing vines. There she is again, the familiar figure of woman in her all-time duality: earth mother and household drudge.

Archaeological treasures employing such motifs have been unearthed in several Mississippian sites. The Spiro Mound complex yielded a particularly rich supply—even after the Pocala Mining Company had ransacked and then dynamited it. As it turned out, Forrest Clements had been too pessimistic in his original appraisal.

Used as a drinking cup, this engraved conch shell is one of possibly more than 500 such objects recovered from Spiro. The intricate design, shown in full form in the drawing below, represents either a birdman deity or a human dressed in a falcon costume and mask and striking a ritual dancing pose.

BARE-BONES EVIDENCE OF THE MIXED BLESSINGS OF A SETTLED LIFE

As the Mississippian culture emerged between AD 800 and 1000, corn became the prevailing agricultural crop. Organized agriculture had distinct advantages over the uncertainty of scrounging a precarious living from the wild. Indeed, farming communities helped foster the rise of the great Mississippian chiefdoms.

But bioarchaeologists specializing in the analysis of human remains have found evidence that this transition also adversely affected the health of some Mississippians.

For one thing, the greater population density of farming communities brought an upsurge in communicable diseases. Skeletons found at Dickson Mounds, Illinois, demonstrate that two types of bone inflammation, periostitis and osteomyelitis, doubled in incidence during the transitional period from the old hunter-gatherer way of life to farming.

More profound evidence exists of the malnutrition that could result from a diet that—while not entirely forsaking wild foods—relied primarily on corn, which is high in carbohydrates but low in protein and certain essential amino acids. In one study, only 0.4 to 7.8 percent of hunter-gatherer teeth had cavities, whereas 4.5 to 43.4 percent of teeth from corn eaters were decayed *(top right)*. And the grooved surfaces of some *(bottom right)* indicate that corn-based diets could hinder enamel growth.

Bones, too, record dietary insufficiencies, with those from some agricultural populations shorter and smaller in circumference—a condition attributed by some scientists to a lack of protein and by others, paradoxically, to improved living standards *(sidebar, far right)*. More certain signs of malnutrition are found in the fourfold increase in Dickson Mounds specimens of porotic hyperostosis *(below)*, perforated bone tissue often associated with iron-deficiency anemia—induced by phytate, a chemical that inhibits iron absorption and that is found, not surprisingly, in corn.

Porotic hyperostosis, the filigree of bone perforations in the sockets of this skull, was caused by marrow expanding to produce more red blood cells, possibly in response to anemia brought on by a corn-rich diet.

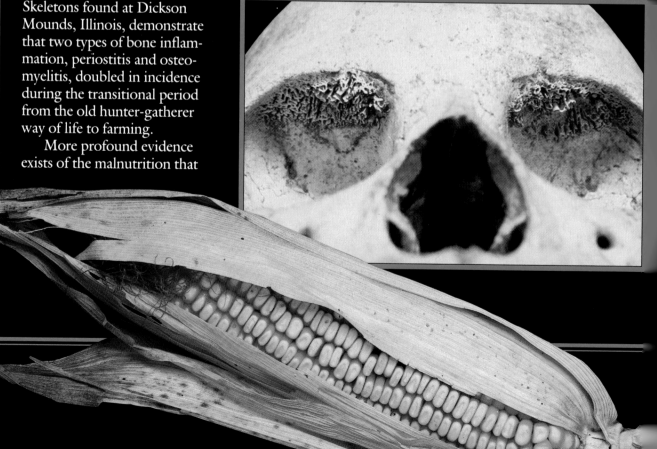

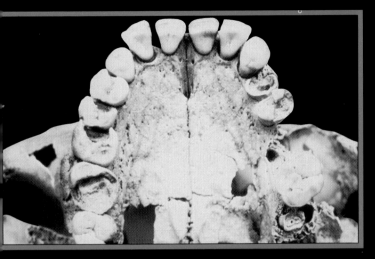

The teeth of a skull dating from the Mississippian agricultural period show a high incidence of decay, most likely the result of a carbohydrate-intense corn diet. Teeth recovered from preagricultural sites generally have only a fraction as many cavities, the benefit of the more varied—if harder-won—range of foods eaten by hunter-gatherers.

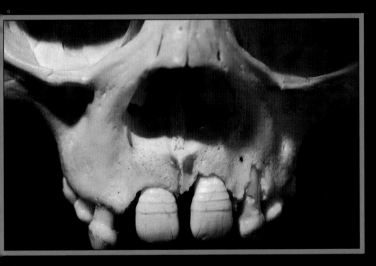

The incisors of a juvenile skull show ridged surface formations—hypoplasias—that indicate disruptions in the normal pattern of enamel development. Scientists conjecture that malnutrition and disease in communities relying on corn for their nourishment could have caused the physiological stresses resulting in such abnormal patterns of enamel growth.

SIGNS OF THE HUNTER'S WEARY LIFE

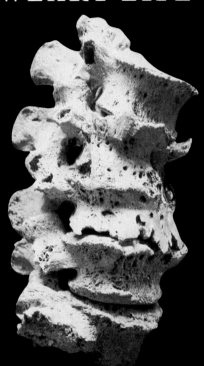

Although the skeletal record dramatically illustrates the malnutrition brought on by a diet that emphasized corn, it also provides evidence that many postagricultural Mississippians led lives free of some of the hardships their ancestors faced.

The physical stress of the hunter-gatherer life shows clearly in preagricultural bones. Vertebrae (*above*) and joints exhibit the wear and tear of osteoarthritis—a condition also found to a greater extent in the skeletons of men, who performed the more strenuous hunting activities.

Even the decrease in bone size found in agricultural sites may indicate that life had become easier rather than that the diet was poorer, since larger,

On closer inspection, Clements saw that the looters' final blast had cracked open part of the main cone to reveal a glimpse of the internal structure: layer upon layer of compacted dirt and clay, untouched, suggesting the possibility that the earth might surrender yet more artifacts. His hopes rose; a salvage operation, at least, was indicated.

Using the profile system—comparable to slicing through a multitiered cake—Clements and his fieldworkers made a series of cuts from top to bottom and saw burials and artifacts embedded in the soil at all levels. "The entire mound was a funerary edifice," he commented afterward, "containing an estimated 900 interments with burial goods, and the proportion of specimens found in the central feature can only be a small part of the total." Like Kelly at Ocmulgee, he had found a stack of mounds within a mound. In their haste, the burrowers had left a sizable quantity of undamaged artifacts for scientists to compare with findings from other Mississippian sites, among them the Cahokia, the only urban—or proto-urban—community in pre-Columbian North America.

Here and there, the ruins of Mississippian life lie bare to the eye, most poignantly in what remains of prehistoric Cahokia, Illinois, about six miles east of the Mississippi in the most fertile of flood plains. No one knows what the inhabitants called their town; the name "Cahokia" derives from a subgroup of the Illini tribe encountered by the French in that area in the late 1600s.

More than a century later, French Trappist monks nonchalantly planted vegetable gardens and fruit trees on the terraces of Cahokia's largest mound, which measures 700 feet by 1,080 feet at its base and rises to a height of 100 feet. The monks' presence here inadvertently gave rise to the name by which the pyramid is known

Reconstructed in 1985, this ring of cedar posts known as a woodhenge apparently served as a solar calendar for Cahokians; viewed from the center, certain poles align with the sun on the solstices and the equinoxes. Other markers may have denoted festival dates—or, possibly, simply served to complete the circle.

The painting above suggests what Cahokia probably looked like in its heyday, viewed from the southwest. Besides Monks Mound, the stockaded central plaza includes the mortuary mound—where deceased members of the elite were apparently prepared for interment—and its adjacent burial mound, a field used possibly for playing a game called chunkey, and numerous smaller platforms for temples or elite residences. Beyond the stockade, ponds have formed in some of the so-called borrow pits, excavations that supplied earth for building mounds.

1 Monks Mound
2 Chunkey field
3 Mortuary mound
4 Burial mound
5 Mound 72
6 Borrow pits
7 Woodhenge

today. Standing today upon Monks Mound, the largest of its kind north of Mexico and the most ambitious earthen construction in the New World, even a casual observer can recapture something of what has gone before. Much of the detritus of centuries has been cleared, opening a window onto a community that emerged around AD 900 and began to fade into obscurity some time after 1300. By 1500 the disappearance was complete.

Centuries later, another culture—in the form of the great westward migration of American pioneers—arrived and inevitably began to intrude upon the site as farmers plowed up the land and made other modifications to it. Archaeologists came too, during the early years of transformation, and found scattered bones and pottery. Work continued over the years, but not until the early 1960s, when plans for Interstate 255 threatened a massive assault on Cahokia, did professional archaeologists launch a desperate attempt to save it. In the next few years, racing ahead of the bulldozers, they not only excavated many mounds packed with artifacts but also succeeded in rerouting the highway to bypass much of the historic area.

Since then, little digging has been done; in all probability, very little will be—with good reason. Starting in 1984, a team of researchers from Southern Illinois University at Edwardsville has been exploring Cahokia with a noninvasive form of archaeology. High-tech instruments read what lies beneath the surface of the soil without disturbing it. In a new remote-sensing procedure, an electromagnetic conductivity meter induces a current to flow into the ground and measure the porosity and electrical properties of the subsoil contents. Is there solid earth beneath, a sand ridge, or a marsh? A palisade, a house, or a buried platform mound?

The device locates anomalies and suggests their nature. "It doesn't always tell you what's there," says a researcher, "but it does tell you that there's something different beneath the surface and gives some indication of what it might be." Core samples have borne out the locations of buried mounds and palisades indicated by the conductivity readings, suggesting that scientists could possibly map unseen Cahokia without having to dig it up. The findings point to a pattern of landscape alteration by the Cahokians themselves that is much more extensive

A figure of great importance, this occupant of Mound 72 at Cahokia lies on an opulent bed—thousands upon thousands of carved conch-shell beads, each with a hole drilled in its center. Archaeologists' strings form a reference grid of 20-inch squares; the arrow points north.

and sophisticated than was previously thought. As the work proceeds, Cahokia reasserts its previous magnitude and complexity through remote sensors connected to aboveground computers.

In its heyday, Cahokia once encompassed nearly six square miles and included 120 mounds. About half of these survive in more or less their original shape. Some few are conical or ridge-topped and show evidence of having been used for ceremonial burials, but most

have platform tops. Cahokia clearly was a major political and religious center, with a population far greater than the entire Natchez nation in its prime. Moreover, the core of the primary settlement was more than a collection of mounds for the sole use of the elite. Studies indicate that the houses of less illustrious citizens used to stand in rows, arranged about open plazas. Residents cultivated their own small garden plots. Larger fields of cultivated corn and other crops spread throughout the surrounding flood plains.

At the height of Cahokia's glory, about AD 1100, the occupants built a wooden stockade some 12 to 15 feet high around the 300-acre central area, either to protect the ceremonial precinct and its aristocracy from attack or to form a physical barrier between the different rankings of society. The stockade might also have ensured a refuge for the entire population in time of danger. Whatever its purpose, the Cahokians rebuilt it three times before the town was abandoned, each time using about 15,000 new logs.

But the dominating feature was Monks Mound. Covering more than 14 acres at its base, it still rises in a series of four tiers, or terraces. It took about 22 million cubic feet of earth and 300 years of building in stages to achieve its ultimate size. The finished mound was topped with an impressive wooden building measuring 105 feet long, 48 feet wide, and about 50 feet high, almost certainly the official residence of Cahokia's ruler, from which he conducted ceremonies and official business.

From their studies, archaeologists can re-create the panorama the chief beheld: a creek close by with trees growing on the banks, the Mississippi some six miles distant, and rich prairie beyond. Down below lay a broad central plaza more or less encircled by simple houses with clay-plastered pole frames and thatched roofs, a stockade wall, and more than one hundred mounds, including a pair of considerable size though nothing like so large as the chief's mound.

Although, thanks to the diligence of the archaeologists, the settlement has gradually revealed itself in many of its physical details, its citizens are still an enigma. No single individual has left a name, a mark, a message. Clues found beneath the surface reveal only the surface life of Cahokia's inhabitants, and in some cases their approximate rank, but never their identity or motivations.

It is assumed, however, that because the Cahokians lived near navigable water, they must have had frequent contact with other Indians. Articles recovered from Mound 72 attest to a busy com-

THE MYSTERIES AND DELIGHTS OF PIPE SMOKING

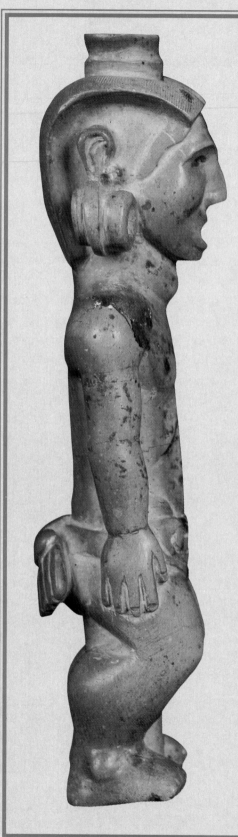

From the evidence of Adena, Hopewell, and Mississippian burials, a pipe must have been among a man's proudest possessions, an object well worth taking to the grave with him. With the growth of each culture, pipes developed their own characteristic shapes, motifs, and sizes.

The discovery of stone pipes in North America dating back to 2500 BC reveals that smoking was practiced even then. Just what significance it held for pre-Columbian peoples, however, can only be deduced from information about later Indians.

Judging from accounts of early explorers traveling near the Great Lakes, the Indians of the region smoked some 27 different plant species, from shredded willow bark to goldenrod flowers. Those to the southeast favored a variant of the tobacco plant.

Smoking apparently had social, supernatural, and healing purposes. And since smoke was associated with fire, a sacred element, it would have been seen as a purifier. In some post-Columbian smoking rituals, to-

Perhaps representing a dwarf, this figure on a 7.8-inch-long Adena pipe from Ohio, dating to the Early Woodland Period (500 BC to AD 1), shows an Adena fascination with deformity. The neck is marked by a large goiter, the result of an iodine deficiency.

bacco smoke was blown in the four cardinal directions. Councils started with a pipe passed to all present, and strangers were welcomed in similar fashion.

Craftsmen manufactured pipes with exquisite care. Using a variety of materials, including sandstone, hematite, and pipestone, they carved, filed, and polished their wares to perfection. In choosing meaningful subjects, they gave full play to their artistic imaginations, as these examples, shown actual size, suggest.

Adena pipes, among the earliest, evolved from tubular shapes into animal forms and on occasion, as at left, even into human effigies. Hopewell pipes are distinguished by their so-called platform bottoms; they generally display thin, curved stems and bowls carved with animals that doubtless functioned as symbols, expressed magical qualities, or had mythical significance. Mississippian pipes, which are sometimes quite large, often depict humans engaged in various activities. While most pipes would have been passed around and smoked ritualistically, some of the Mississippian specimens are plainly too heavy to have been shifted from hand to hand easily. Instead, the participants would have had to come to the pipes themselves to take a drag.

Surprisingly elaborate for its four-inch length, this Hopewell pipe features a roseate spoonbill perched on a fish, whose head functions as the mouthpiece. The Hopewell must have regarded the pink-feathered bird, a species limited to tropical climes, as a curiosity. Found in Ohio, the pipe is believed to date from between 100 BC and AD 400.

Smoking a pipe with an animal head, the figure of a man in this imaginative design becomes the pipe itself, with the hole for the mouthpiece in the front. This Mississippian example, dated between AD 800 and 1500 and carved from redstone, stands 8.5 inches high, has a 10-inch-long base, and weighs 7 pounds 12 ounces.

merce. In close proximity to ancient human bones lay objects not native to the area: arrowheads traceable to Oklahoma, Tennessee, and Arkansas, tons of small ornaments made from Gulf of Mexico conch shells, mica from North Carolina, and rolled sheets of copper used for decorative breastplates believed to have come from the vicinity of Lake Superior.

With a little imagination, it is easy to conjure up a picture of life in Cahokia during its period of greatest development. The plaza, lying convenient to the creek, draws travelers from distant societies who offer their shells and copper, as well as furs, hides and dried meats. Cahokia's own laborers are on hand with flintlike stones for hoe blades and salt from nearby springs. Others display wares fashioned in their workshops: tools and arrowheads, dressed hides, decorative pots, and woven baskets, ornaments hammered out of imported copper, bracelets and pendants of pearly shell beads.

On other days there might be a festival in the plaza, or a sporting event. The game of choice is *chunkey*. This is an activity requiring great vigor and skill, and only the warrior class participates. Like some prehistoric and demanding form of hockey crossed with quoits, the sport requires each player to roll a heavy stone disk as far as possible, then quickly throw a spear at the point where he estimates the disk will roll to a stop.

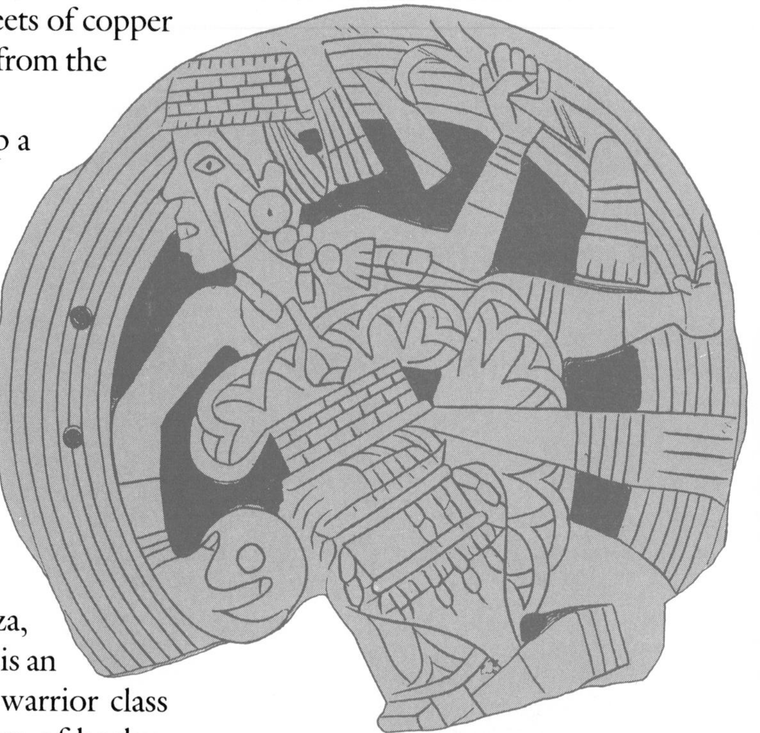

At most times the shadows cast by the great mounds dominate the scene. And yet there is something else that is always there, something whose workings are a mystery to most common folk. These are arrangements of red cedar posts in large circles, whose postholes archaeologists have unearthed, creations that have to do with the administration of greater Cahokia by the aristocracy. The chiefs or priests use such circles—called woodhenges by some—to track the shifting seasons by observing the sun. From a central observation point, they can sight along the posts and line them up with the rising sun at certain times of the year: the equinoxes and the winter and summer solstices. To the ruling elite, it is an advantage to have knowledge of the seasons—and the annual, inevitable floods—through an accurate solar calendar. Armed with such information, they can demonstrate to the uninitiated masses their control of time, and tie the schedule of feasts and rituals to the cosmic order.

The drawing above, reproduced from a shell gorget, depicts a chunkey player in full regalia, clutching the stone disk he will roll in one hand and the stick he will hurl at the spot where he expects the stone to come to a stop. As is indicated by the elaborate costume, chunkey players were evidently highly regarded and may have played some symbolic role in the society. Shown opposite is an actual chunkey stone, measuring six inches in diameter and with a typical concave face.

For two days each year, then as now, the rising sun appears to claim the city as its own. On those days of equinox it bursts up spectacularly from behind the great mound of the chief, as if the mound itself were giving birth to the blazing ball of light.

But there may at one time have been a darker side to Cahokian life, one that did not celebrate the sun. The excavation of Mound 72 laid bare numbers of ceremonial and sacrificial burials in several mass graves. Of the individuals interred, at least three appear to have been important personages who died at different times. Nearly all the skeletal remains indicate funereal sacrifice. The central figure of the main burial grouping, a male about 45 years old, lay on a carpet of tens of thousands of shell beads with an assorted selection of grave goods. Near him was a pit full of skeletal attendants, consisting of four men whose heads and hands were unaccountably missing—but whose arms, curiously, were linked—and 53 women between the ages of 15 and 25.

Several other mass burials—totaling nearly 300—were found close by, in the vicinity of splendidly laid-out figures. It seems that Cahokia's rulers, like the chiefs of the Natchez, could and did take their cohorts with them. Could all these apparently healthy people possibly have gone willingly? Did they all sincerely believe in a glorious afterlife in the Upper World? Or were the skeletons those of captives or slaves? And why so many young women?

There are, as yet, no answers.

For reasons still unknown, Cahokia's population began to decline after AD 1300, and the town dwindled to a village. By 1500 it had been abandoned altogether. Its greatness may have been its undoing. Quite possibly Cahokia depleted the natural resources of its immediate environment or used them at a rate faster than they could be replaced. Land-office surveys of the early 1800s—when the area supported a much smaller population—indicate a paucity of forests in the wet bottom lands. Centuries earlier, thousands of people over hundreds of years had felled the trees for buildings, stockades, and firewood—all the while diminishing the habitat of the animals they hunted for food. Cahokians would have had to go farther and farther afield to seek the materials they needed to sustain the lifestyle they had grown accustomed to.

At the same time, the expanding township was probably experiencing typical urban problems such as overpopulation and inadequate sanitation. Close quarters may well have encouraged epidemics long before Europeans brought their own exotic diseases to ravage native peoples. Skeletal remains indicate that tuberculosis, blastomycosis—a fungal disorder—and syphilis were present; not in enough magnitude, certainly, to wipe out a civilization, but perhaps in enough to spur an exodus to healthier climes.

It is also possible that worldwide climatic changes, beginning in the 13th century, might have led to a lowering of temperatures, floods, or droughts that the guardians of the solar calendar could not anticipate. Unexpected and unexplained natural calamities may have fomented social unrest as well as disrupted the agricultural cycle. Whatever the complex of causes for their leaving, the Cahokians did not depart en masse; archaeological evidence points to a gradual exodus over a period of two centuries. Thus, too, did the other Mississippian settlements fade, prodded sometimes by foreign guns and disease, or brought low by nature and even by their own ultimate lack of understanding of its delicate balance.

There remain quiet places today where the platform mounds are buried beneath wild grass and shadowy trees, almost as if they were natural formations. In a sense, they are.

KEYS TO THE UNIVERSE

Midwestern and eastern portions of the United States witnessed an extraordinary flowering of culture between the years AD 800 and 1500. The mighty Mississippians, or Temple Mound Builders, recruited artisans to create small works of art that were at the same time badges of chiefly office and the tangible embodiment of popular belief. And it was these that their owners saw fit to take to the grave with them, perhaps to aid them in the afterlife.

To 20th-century eyes the objects are mysterious, sometimes eerie. So baffling are they, so ubiquitous are the themes and motifs observed throughout the Mississippians' enormous domain, stretching from the Gulf Coast to the Great Lakes and from Florida to Oklahoma, that early scholars postulated the existence of a widespread religious cult. Yet, as far as can be determined, there never was such a cult. What the Mississippians shared instead was a chal-

lenging and bewildering natural world, one that required constant effort to explain the inexplicable and reconcile the irreconcilable. Obscure though their work may sometimes be, it expresses their beliefs in striking fashion.

Archaeologists studying that work have drawn upon the oral traditions of Indians postdating the Mississippians to understand and interpret it. They see the thinking of these vanished people rooted in the concept of a universe consisting of three worlds. Two of them, the harmonious Upper World and the infernal Under World, were locked in perpetual conflict. Sandwiched between them was This World, the less-than-perfect habitat of humans. The marine-shell gorget above doubtless symbolizes the Upper World, with the cross standing for the four cardinal directions converging on the sun. Just who the figures represent with their large eyes and painted or tattooed faces no one knows.

AN UPPER WORLD OF STABILITY AND LIGHT

Rising abruptly from the flat land, the slope-sided temple mounds aspire toward the sun, principal deity of the Mississippians. In the sun's glittering realm, the Upper World, all things animate and inanimate were larger, mightier, and endowed with greater powers than in the mundane world of humans. How pale, therefore, even the sacred fire of the temple must have seemed compared with the sun's great blaze.

For these earthbound people, the Upper World epitomized stability, order, predictability. Yet the Upper World was not complete: Just as the Mississippians needed fire to live, so did they need its opposite, water, which issued from springs of the shadowy and mysterious Under World.

As the mediators between these conflicting spheres, the chief and other members of the elite would have interpreted the old beliefs for their people and striven to maintain, through ritual and ceremonies, the delicate balance between the opposing forces of order and chaos. Set apart from all others, they wore and used the objects reproduced here.

Both the ceramic bottle at left and the shell gorget above display a quintessential symbol of the Upper World and its ordered symmetry: the combined circle-and-cross motif representing the sun and the four cardinal points—or the solar deity as embodied in the earthly chief. The more detailed gorget compresses a major statement of chiefly authority into its 4¼-inch diameter by enclosing this motif in a square representing a royal litter attended by four woodpeckers, symbolizing the sky and military might.

This ritual feline head, with little more than eyes and teeth remaining, displays an Upper World forked-eye motif modeled after falcon-eye markings and thought to represent exceptional vision. The piece is of copper, a metal that enjoyed high status among the Mississippians, partly for its rarity. The ore came from distant Great Lakes sources.

The stone ear spool at right is a ceremonial adornment whose use is as much a mystery as its design. The falcon-eye marking is curiously at odds with the half-closed eye and the bared teeth of the open mouth, both of which suggest the face of a dead man. It is possible that the motif depicts a trophy head and symbolizes the concept of mortality.

Discovered in 1906 by a Missouri farmer while plowing, this falcon-headed repoussé copper plaque is as much an emblem of war as of the Upper World. The design of the 13-inch-high figure was hammered in from the reverse side. The plaque was intended to be worn upright on the front of the head.

MIRROR TO THE UNDER WORLD: REFLECTIONS OF DARKNESS, HORROR, AND DEATH

In contrast to the lofty brightness of the Upper World, the Under World loomed as a dark and dank morass of madness and disorder, the lair of unnaturally large lizards, giant frogs, and slithering creatures epitomized by the rattlesnake and other reptiles. Even more fearsome would have been ghosts, cannibals, and witches—all of whom could sidle into This World through waterways and caves, there to wreak havoc in the lives of its inhabitants.

Archaeologists can only guess at meanings, but they are aided by what they know about other, later Indian cultures. The monster called Uktena by the Cherokees, for example, had the wings of an Upper World bird, the antlers of an earthly deer, and the scaly body of a typical Under World serpent. This blurring of the boundaries between realms is evident in many Mississippian artifacts that depict more than one world or one theme on a single object. The Under World was itself a paradox in that it represented not only the dark, death-dealing side of the cosmos but also the fertility of the soil, upon which all life depended.

Found near Cahokia, Illinois, this eight-inch bauxite sculpture, seen from two angles, links motifs. The woman tilling the vines sprouting from the serpent illustrates fertility, while her bared teeth suggest the expression of one who has died.

Objects crafted from marine shells native to the Gulf of Mexico and Florida were highly prized by the Mississippian elite as symbols of high status and spiritual value. This engraved four-inch disk (left), cut from a conch shell and worn as a neckpiece, depicts an Under World water spider.

Conch-shell cups were associated exclusively with the highest-ranking leaders and may have been used for consumption of a ritual drink. The engraved cup at right shows four serpentine monsters within the Upper World context of cross and circle.

In Mississippian belief the lowly turtle was as much an Under World creature as were the alligator and the snake, but was depicted as benign. The ceramic turtle-effigy vessel shown here, its use unknown, was found in Arkansas.

MISSISSIPPIAN WARFARE: THE PATH TO UPWARD MOBILITY AND GREATNESS

Warfare meant much to the Mississippians, for more than mere survival was at stake. Whether they knew it or not, fighting their enemies would have been a means of assuring a satisfied and socially cohesive community, constantly renewed by its strength and vigor. Going to war gave members of the elite the opportunity to reaffirm their own position at the top of the social ladder by their brave deeds on the battlefield; for lesser warriors, skill in combat would have offered stepping-stones to recognition and higher status. Enemy heads, taken as trophies, became eloquent testimonials of such prowess.

Maintaining a stable society through military success would have necessitated good relations with all forces of the cosmos and constant visual reminders of war's glories. Of the numerous bellicose symbols employed in Mississippian art, one of the most prevalent is the birdman, who could rise above all others and was often depicted as a warrior with the head of an Upper World falcon.

A 9.7-inch human-effigy pipe (left) *found at Spiro, Oklahoma, portrays a figure in a headdress, either a warrior severing the prized head of an enemy captured in battle or an executioner decapitating a sacrificial victim.*

The shell gorget above manages to pack an array of warfare motifs into its 3.9-inch frame. The warrior figure, sporting an arrow in his hair and the forked eye of the falcon on his face, holds a war club in one hand and a trophy head in the other.

The skull-and-bone symbol inevitably associated with death is clearly illustrated on this 4.6-inch ceramic cup found in Moundville, Alabama. The skeletal motifs may stand for war trophies or ancestral relics, perhaps objects of veneration.

A large fragmented copper repoussé plate found at Etowah, Georgia, depicts a birdman dancer, with war club, arrow, and trophy head.

UPTURNED PALMS AND STARING EYES: STRANGE SYMBOLS OF THE UNKNOWN

Despite the best efforts of archaeologists and cultural anthropologists, certain objects left behind by the Mississippians resist final interpretation. The symbols are blatant and compelling—skulls and bones; stylized, eerie eyes peering from the palms of hands; crosses that take the shape of swastikas; entangled birdmen; brooding godlike figures—but just how these were regarded and understood may never be known with any certainty.

One mysterious motif, the open hand, appears over and over again. Does it signify wisdom, peace, or has it a more sinister meaning? During excavations at Spiro, Oklahoma, a carefully buried pottery jar filled with hand bones turned up, but no one could tell whether they had come from sacrifices, prisoners taken in battle, or the honored dead. What is certain is that all the pieces shown here, with the exception of the outsize pipe in the lower right-hand corner opposite, were used for adornment. The twin holes drilled along their edges—through which a leather thong or a cord could be threaded—is the evidence of that.

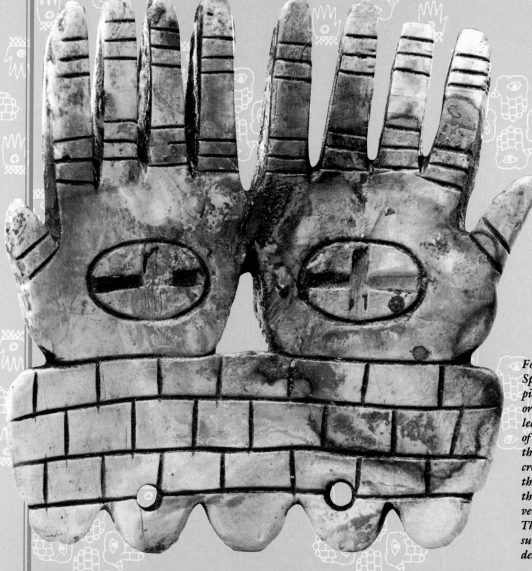

Found in the Craig Mound at Spiro, this detailed marine-shell piece served either as a pendant or as a headdress tied to a leather band. The combination of symbols—the hand, the eye in the palm, the circle and the cross—suggests a funerary theme. The hands may represent those of warriors or other revered members of the society. The eyes might symbolize the sun god or his powerful earthly descendant, the chief.

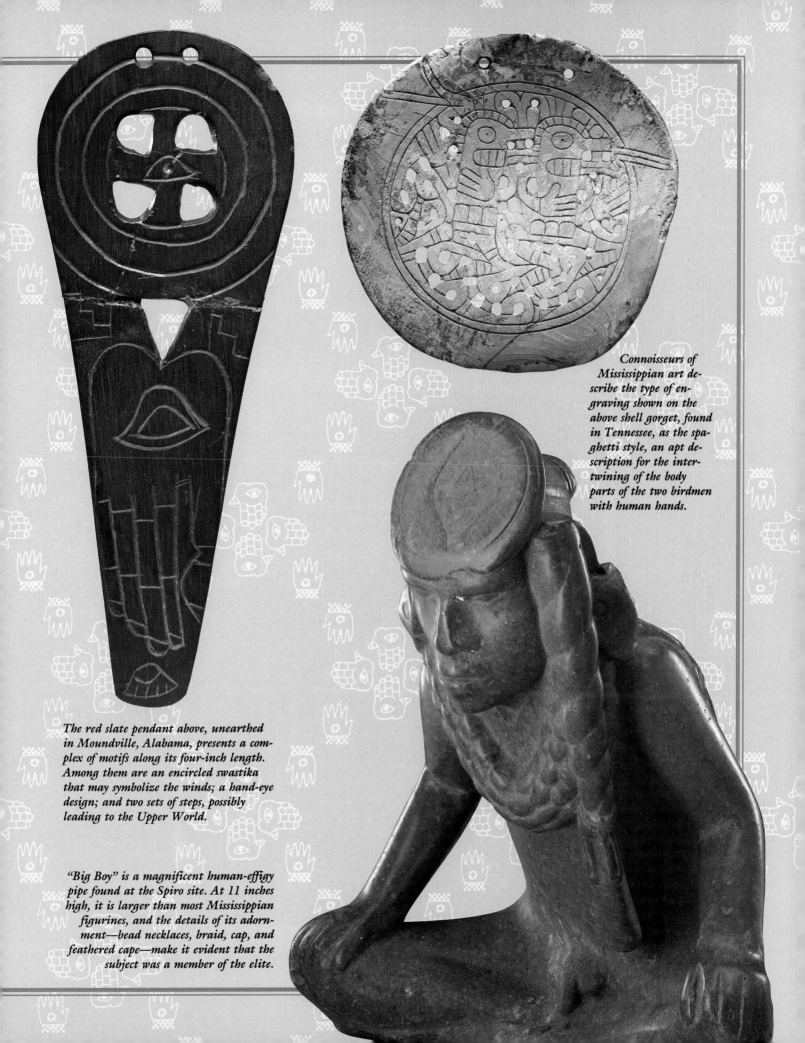

Connoisseurs of Mississippian art describe the type of engraving shown on the above shell gorget, found in Tennessee, as the spaghetti style, an apt description for the intertwining of the body parts of the two birdmen with human hands.

The red slate pendant above, unearthed in Moundville, Alabama, presents a complex of motifs along its four-inch length. Among them are an encircled swastika that may symbolize the winds; a hand-eye design; and two sets of steps, possibly leading to the Upper World.

"Big Boy" is a magnificent human-effigy pipe found at the Spiro site. At 11 inches high, it is larger than most Mississippian figurines, and the details of its adornment—bead necklaces, braid, cap, and feathered cape—make it evident that the subject was a member of the elite.

THE SOUTHWEST: THRIVING IN A PITILESS DOMAIN

Richard Wetherill and his brother-in-law Charlie Mason had passed a wet morning tracking stray cattle in a steady snowfall near the Wetherill ranch in Colorado's Mancos Valley, not far from the southwestern landmark known as the Four Corners—where Arizona, Utah, Colorado, and New Mexico meet. By noon on this December day in 1888 they had reached the top of the brush-fringed tableland called Mesa Verde. The mesa's sheer cliffs were pierced by a succession of steep-walled canyons, and as the two cowboys dismounted to rest their horses they realized that they had wandered to the rim of a canyon they had not seen before.

Walking to the edge of the cliff and peering through the snow to the far side of the gorge half a mile away, they caught sight of something that took their breath away. Miragelike, built into a long, deep slash in the sandstone wall, was a silent, ghostly city of cliff houses. Wetherill and Mason had seen cliff dwellings on Mesa Verde's flanks before, but never such as these. The masonry structures were piled atop one another on an elaborate series of terraces roofed by natural rock. Windows like unseeing eyes dotted the stone walls, and a tapering three-story tower stood near the center of the precarious settlement. The entire ruin, which Wetherill soon named Cliff Palace, looked spacious enough to house several hundred people.

The two men improvised a ladder to help them clamber down

Filled with lost meaning, a 600-year-old petroglyph on an outcrop south of Santa Fe, New Mexico, shows a masked Anasazi man wearing an eagle feather and carrying what may be a ceremonial staff.

to the canyon floor, then climbed the slippery slope beyond to explore their discovery. Wide-eyed, they shuffled through eerily dark and dusty rooms where no one had trod for more than 600 years. Then they began to find things: a stone ax lashed to a wooden handle, corncobs, pottery bowls, and large jars. Mason got the impression that the cliff dwellers had departed in haste. But at least three never left. Their skeletons lay among the rubble.

Flushed with excitement, the cowboys returned to their horses and separated to see what else they could find in the daylight that remained. Mason came up empty, but by nightfall Wetherill had discovered a smaller, better-preserved cliff dwelling in another canyon. The next day they chanced upon a third one, a 70-room cave colony with a tower higher than that at Cliff Palace.

Wetherill, the oldest of five sons of a Quaker rancher who had migrated west from Pennsylvania, was hooked. The ruins thrilled him in a way he could never articulate; he knew only that he wanted to see and learn more. Eventually he became obsessed with his quest, acquiring thousands of artifacts of the people he named Anasazi (a Navajo word alternately translated as "ancient ones" and "enemy ancestors") for museums in the United States and Europe. In his own

Crouched at their encampment close by the Anasazi ruins of Pueblo Bonito in New Mexico's Chaco Canyon, members of the 1896 Hyde Exploring Expedition— Richard Wetherill (right), archaeologist George Pepper, freighter Orian Buck, and an unidentified Navajo helper—sift through dirt taken from a room of the pueblo. Among their finds at the site were more than 2,000 turquoise beads (above) that had been stowed in a basket as part of a funeral trove.

dogged, self-taught way, he would become an important pioneer in the study of the ancient peoples of the American Southwest.

A century and a half of both amateur and professional archaeology, going back beyond Wetherill to the military travelers who described the spectacular ruins at Chaco Canyon in New Mexico in 1849, has produced a set of qualified conclusions about the region's prehistoric Indians—qualified because new information and interpretations continue to emerge. Settled doctrine has proved elusive; as one writer on the subject cautions, with southwestern prehistory "you begin each sentence with 'maybe' and end it with 'probably.'"

With such reservations in mind, most scholars posit that three major cultures occupied the Southwest during roughly the same time period that the Hopewell and Mississippian cultures developed in the eastern United States. The Anasazi, concentrated near the Four Corners, are the best known, and their intriguing pueblo ruins and cliff dwellings are the best preserved and the most exhaustively studied. In fact, the ruins discovered by Wetherill and others who followed him have so stirred Americans' fancy that the diverse pre-Columbian peoples of the Southwest are still sometimes lumped together as "Cliff Dwellers," a catchy—but less than accurate—label.

The Mogollon people, the second major group, lived mainly amid the mountains of that name along the central Arizona-New Mexico border. Late in their history the Mogollon and the Anasazi became more alike. But early on, one Mogollon district made a distinctive contribution, fashioning what is generally regarded as the region's most beautiful and sophisticated craft product, the pottery known as Mimbres black-on-white (*pages 98-99*).

The third group, the Hohokam, was dealt the harshest environment, the Sonoran Desert and the meagerly watered valleys of south central Arizona. They grappled with aridity just as modern desert dwellers do, by building elaborate irrigation systems to water their crops, despite the fact that, like all the early Indians of the Southwest, they dug without metal tools and moved large quantities of dirt without the wheel or beasts of burden. Archaeologists have identified at least four minor cultures in the region as well, two of which—the Fremont in Utah and the Sinagua in northern Arizona—are better known than the others.

The scholarly consensus begins to fray on such questions as

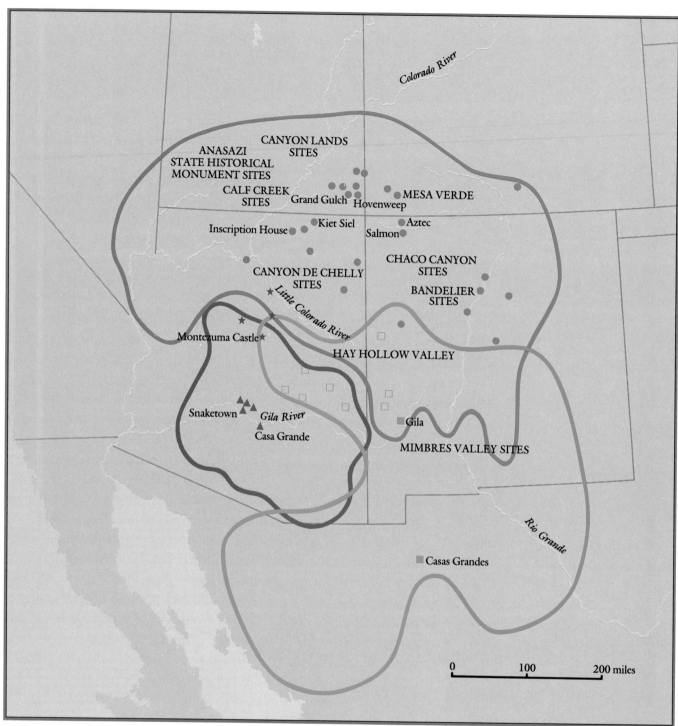

- ● Anasazi sites
- ■ Mogollon sites
- ☐ Western Pueblo sites
     (Mogollon descendants)
- ▲ Hohokam sites
- ★ Sinagua sites

This map of the southwestern United States and northern Mexico shows the regions of influence of one minor and three major prehistoric Indian cultures that existed separately for more than a thousand years, until approximately AD 1450. The Anasazi (red) lived throughout the Four Corners states of Colorado, Utah, Arizona, and New Mexico. (Areas identified with capital letters denote the presence of many Anasazi sites.) The Mogollon and their descendants (green) occupied the Arizona-New Mexico border area and northern Mexico, while the Hohokam (blue) toiled in the deserts of south central Arizona, south of a small region that was inhabited by the Sinagua (purple). Although cultures occasionally intermingled where boundaries are shown to overlap, it was also the case that different cultures occupied the same area at different times.

how long these societies lasted (an average estimate is about 1,000 years), where they came from originally, and, most intriguing of all, what ultimately became of them. The Mogollon and the Hohokam began to lose their singular identities sometime between 1200 and 1450, but they did not disappear. Indians with similar customs were living in the same areas when the first Europeans came on the scene, and researchers are satisfied that a link exists between the ancient Mogollon, Anasazi, and Hohokam peoples and modern tribes including the Zuni, Hopi, Pima, and Papago.

If the main theme of southwestern archaeology sometimes seems to be the persistence of unanswered questions—how the ball courts found in Hohokam country, for example, are connected with similar structures associated with more advanced Mexican cultures such as the Maya—the main impression left by a study of these peoples is of their extraordinary cultural longevity and gritty adaptability to daunting conditions, mixed with whiffs of legend and magic that linger in their dust. As the University of New Mexico anthropologist Alfonso Ortiz puts it, they made of their environment "a humanized landscape suffused with ancient meanings, myths, and mysteries."

For Richard Wetherill, at least in the early years of his career as an explorer of Anasazi ruins, the principal attraction was not so much myths and mysteries as dollars and cents. Together with his brothers John, Al, and Clayton, and his brother-in-law Charlie Mason, he converted his stock of artifacts into cold, hard cash *(page 112)*. But while searching for more objects to sell in a relatively small cliff house north of Johnson Canyon, he and Mason made a particularly awe-inspiring discovery. After removing a large rock sealing a doorway and breaking through an interior wall, they came upon what looked like a sepulcher for Anasazi warriors.

Five skeletons lay on the ground, with 17 arrows across their skulls. Four bowls rested between the skulls. One large skeleton was stretched out on top of a piece of matting with a bow on one side and a mug and basket—the finest they had seen—on the other. A hollow stick with a six-inch bone point lay nearby. It was the bow, the heaviest they had found, that most impressed Charlie Mason. The bowstring, made of twisted sinews, was "larger than a slate pencil, and he who could draw one of those arrows to the head with such a bow," Mason exclaimed, "must have been a powerful man."

The Quaker cowpunchers were still largely innocent of the

TALKING STONES: GUIDE TO A CULTURAL LANDSCAPE

Of the rich legacies that the ancient cultures of the Southwest have left behind, one of the most eloquent is their art—paintings and carvings rendered on the rocks of their domain. Using mineral colors, or chiseling with stone tools on canyon walls, boulders, and caves, they created images that can be read as a guide to their cultural landscape.

Ceremonial masks, human hands, and figures such as a humpbacked flute player, birds, insects, snakes, game animals, and abstract forms appear over and over again. Archaeologists believe that these are icons of religious ideology that served as aids to ritual.

The paintings are known as pictographs, the carvings as petroglyphs. Scholars often can attribute them to specific peoples—the Anasazi, Hohokam, and Mogollon. Although these cultures influenced one another when they met for trade or during migrations, some groups managed to preserve their own aesthetic modes, as examples of their art on these and the following two pages demonstrate.

Towering above an ancient trade route in Arizona, a cluster of boulders displays numerous petroglyphs superimposed on one another—between AD 200 and 1450—by Hohokam artists.

This Mogollon mask of red and green with stars or crosses for eyes, rendered approximately life-size, was painted on a granite rock at a desert oasis in Hueco Tanks, Texas. Its abstract style is enhanced by a lack of outline.

Concentric circles enclosing decorative geometric designs, in the Jornada Mogollon style, were probably of ritual significance. Between about AD 1000 and 1400, artists pecked them out on the rocks of a ridge top, perhaps a religious site, at Three Rivers, New Mexico.

Tall yuccas rise beside these humans; some think the dots above the heads represent headdresses. To the right of the figures are a bird and a mountain sheep. These petroglyphs were carved on a boulder in Utah, between AD 200 and 500, by the early Anasazi, known as the Basket Makers.

Later Anasazi artists advanced beyond the static figures shown opposite to create more animated ones (above). *In this pictograph found in Utah, the legs are well formed instead of sticklike, and the silhouetted hands are life-size.*

Peoples of the Southwest, from the Archaic tribes of 1000 BC to the contemporary Navajo—and European settlers as well—have cut into the dark face of Newspaper Rock in Utah. Among its images is a man on horseback (upper right) *incised by Utes as recently as the 19th century.*

careful scientific techniques emerging in the nascent discipline of archaeology, but at least they knew that they needed guidance. When they asked the Smithsonian Institution and the Peabody Museum at Harvard for assistance, however, they were turned down flat. Help finally arrived in the summer of 1891 from an unexpected direction. Gustav Eric Adolf Nordenskiöld, the scholarly 23-year-old son of a Swedish baron-cum-scientist-explorer, showed up at the ranch.

Decked out in his borrowed leggings and cowboy hat, the pince-nezed, lavishly mustached Nordenskiöld gamely climbed the nearly vertical canyon walls and studied several ruins. He was the first to realize that the round rooms the Wetherills had thought were storage rooms were actually the ceremonial chambers and meeting places called kivas by the later Hopi. Nordenskiöld was amazed by the careful workmanship evident in the cliff houses' masonry walls, and he discovered small fingerprints in the mortar that led him to believe that the Anasazi plasterers were women. From charred cobs, seeds, and other evidence, he identified the staples of the Anasazi diet as corn, squash, and beans, and he recognized the bird bones found in some sections of the caves as turkey.

The Swede also introduced the Wetherills to stratigraphy, explaining the connection between successive layers of earth and the relative antiquity of artifacts, though the phases of the Anasazi oc-cupation of Mesa Verde were not well understood for some 50 years. Tree-ring dating and other techniques eventually showed a 700-year Anasazi residence in the area ending about 1300 and revealed that the multistory cliff dwellings were used during only the final 100 years.

The Wetherills, meanwhile, em-ployed their newfound exper-tise to assemble another collection of Mesa Verde artifacts for dis-play, rather than for sale, in the Colorado exhibit at the 1893 Chicago World Columbian Exposition. Richard, escorting the exhibit at the request of Colorado officials, became acquainted in Chicago with two wealthy young men who would become his patrons for a decade of archaeology: 20-year-old Talbot Hyde and his 18-year-old broth-er Fred, heirs to the Babbitt Soap Company fortune. Richard con-vinced the Hydes that the first goal of what he expansively christened the Hyde Exploring Expedition should be another cliff-dwelling site he knew at Grand Gulch, near Bluff City in southeastern Utah.

With Nordenskiöld's example still fresh in his mind, Richard was now determined to make his work scientifically respectable. He invented a field form with tidily numbered sections for each important fact about a site. At times his desire to be taken seriously sounded almost poignant. "I want to make myself thoroughly acquainted with the whole Southwest," he wrote to a friend. "But first I must be educated. This is rather a slow process." No longer would he sell his finds to the highest bidder or advertise them, as he once did, as "Aztec relics"; his understanding with the Hydes was that everything would go to the American Museum of Natural History in New York.

Richard Wetherill, his brothers John and Al, and five other men spent four months at Grand Gulch and at two other Utah locales accumulating 1,216 artifacts—including 96 skeletons. Richard was delighted with their success, which, he wrote Talbot Hyde, "surpassed all expectations." It was clear that he had paid attention to Nordenskiöld's lessons in stratigraphy. Three feet below the floor of the Utah cliff houses he found skeletons of what he excitedly declared was a "different race," a people he identified as larger, having baskets but no pottery: "The whole thing is truly wonderful." Richard called them the Basket People, later amended to Basket Makers, and reported that while Cliff Dwellers had bows and arrows, these folk had only the rudimentary spear-propelling weapon called an atlatl.

Some scholars, of course, were dubious. One Harvard professor went so far as to label Richard's Basket Makers a clever hoax designed to inflate "the sales value of his collection if not its credibility." Twenty years later, in 1914, archaeologists working in northern Arizona vindicated Richard by confirming the Basket Makers as an earlier phase of the Anasazi, or Pueblo, culture.

In the summer of 1895, a traveling family of Quaker musicians named Palmer visited the Wetherill ranch and happened to mention a ruin they had been told about in New Mexico's Chaco Canyon, some 140 miles south of Mesa Verde. Richard, who had heard similar rumors, promptly volunteered to take them there, a decision that would both dramatically change his life and lead to one of the first long-term digs of a prehistoric site in the Southwest. The numerous ruined pueblos in the 10-mile-long sandstone canyon had first been described nearly 50 years earlier by an awed U.S. Army lieutenant named James Simpson. The lieutenant had measured the perimeter of the well-preserved, half-moon-shaped settlement called Pueblo Bonito ("beautiful village") at 1,300 feet, and estimated that it had contained as many as 640 rooms in four stories. Simpson had

TIME TOLD BY TREES: CLUES TO THE SOUTHWESTERN PAST

Andrew E. Douglass, an astronomer at the University of Arizona during the early part of the 20th century, tracked back into the golden age of pueblo and cliff-house development, using, as he was fond of saying, the diaries of trees for his guide. By diaries, he meant, of course, tree rings, the concentric record of the wood's annual growth. The rings revealed not only the trees' ages but also climatic conditions during their lifetimes, with seasons of drought or heavy rains showing up as thin or broad rings.

Douglass launched his study because of his interest in sunspots. He theorized that these 11-year cyclical solar disturbances could affect the earth's weather and thus have a direct effect on the width of the growing rings. But as Douglass accumulated data from living Arizona trees,

like the gnarled, ancient piñon used here as a background, he became increasingly fascinated by the linear calendar he was assembling and recognized the need to push beyond the ages of his oldest subjects. In 1923 he began examining wood beams and charcoal from both abandoned and still-inhabited historic Indian sites. In some cases, rings of living trees and those of dead wood matched. But though his chronology went back to AD 1260, Douglass still had many pieces of older wood that did not correspond to dated samples; instead, several overlapped in a sequence of their own. Plainly, what Douglass needed was, as he put it, a Rosetta stone of tree rings to link his two chronologies.

The opportunity came when the cross section of a carbonized pine beam *(below)* revealed that

the tree, chopped down about AD 1380, had begun its life in 1237. When spliced into the chronologies the scientist had already worked out, it extended his dateline, giving him an unbroken record of matching rings for more than 1,200 years. He kept expanding ancient horizons, eventually completing a chronology spanning 1,900 years based on thousands of samples.

Douglass's work revolutionized archaeology in the Southwest, leading to the development of the sciences of dendrochronology, in which archaeologists use tree rings to date structures and sites, and dendroclimatology, the study of the connection between climate and trees. Thus it is possible to say when various pueblos and cliff dwellings, such as Arroyo Hondo *(opposite),* were built and when they were abandoned.

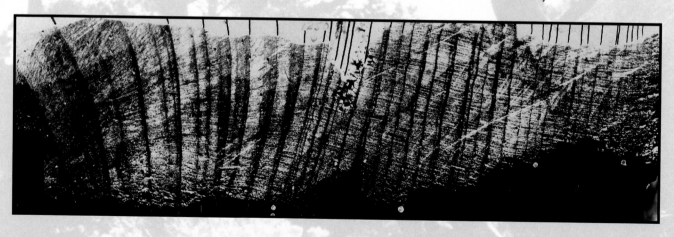

MATCHING THE RINGS: A STORY OF GOOD YEARS AND BAD

Dendrochronology involves taking wood samples from a particular region and determining the ages of the trees by comparing their rings. Here, sample A comes from a tree cut in 1992. Samples B and C are pieces of unknown date. But when their rings are lined up under A's, they match. The year 1985 is common to A and B, 1975 to A, B, and C, and 1965 to B and C. Obtaining the age of each tree now becomes a matter of counting from the outer ring to the core.

Dendrochronology and dendroclimatology have become highly sophisticated tools that can be used to date a pueblo like Arroyo Hondo *(below)* and to establish how many inches of moisture the area received over the lifetime of the pueblo. The data obtained can also be used to show how the population rose and fell with changing conditions.

The ruins of Arroyo Hondo, a pueblo near Santa Fe, New Mexico, occupy a slope 7,100 feet above sea level. Founded around AD 1300, the pueblo was subject to the vagaries of climate. It swelled to almost 100 times its original size when conditions were good, shrank when precipitation declined, and came back to life when the moisture level rose. Tree rings record these wet and dry spells, but only a meticulous and complex statistical analysis of the data would be able to provide figures revealing actual amounts of precipitation.

been particularly dazzled by the Chaco masonry, so "beautifully diminutive and true," he wrote, that it reminded him of "a magnificent piece of mosaic work."

Wetherill, arriving in October with the Palmers, immediately zeroed in on Pueblo Bonito as the arena for his next adventure. His letter to Hyde proposing an expedition brimmed with barely contained exuberance: The ruins were "almost unknown," he had found 11 large pueblos in the canyon already, and all told there might be more than a hundred. The Hydes agreed to subsidize a dig beginning the following summer. But this time there would be an important difference: A scientist and not Richard would be in charge. A 23-year-old Harvard archaeology student named George Pepper was recommended to the Hydes by F. W. Putnam, curator of both the Peabody Museum and the American Museum of Natural History.

Pepper, Wetherill, and a crew of 18 Navajos (whose language Wetherill spoke) began work at Pueblo Bonito in late spring 1896. Though Pepper made it clear that he would leave the manual labor to others and concentrate on recordkeeping, Wetherill was rankled that Pepper was there at all. He complained to Talbot Hyde about what he called Pepper's inefficiency and mentioned, without elaborating, that at one point he had "mutinied" against his youthful superior. Wetherill fretted that Pepper, as a recognized scientist, would take credit for whatever they unearthed.

The finds came steadily as they excavated 18 rooms and one large kiva through the early summer. Then, in August, they made a remarkable series of discoveries. After removing clumps of greasewood shrubs and scraping away a layer of drifted sand, the Navajos reached the top of a buried wall. Two feet below floor level they found a few pieces of turquoise. Digging deeper, they uncovered a cache of 20 perfectly preserved jars and bowls. Two more days of excavation yielded 12 turquoise pendants, 114 jars, and 22 bowls—one of the largest pottery deposits ever found in the Southwest.

In the first of two small rooms adjoining this cache was an even more thrilling discovery, the grave of what clearly appeared to be an important Anasazi personage. A quiver bearing 81 arrows lay near his bones, along with pottery, more than 300 wooden staffs, and a stone bird effigy inlaid with turquoise. The second room held the remains of another high-status individual, whose wrists and ankles were ringed by thick bands of turquoise pendants and beads. Two additional pendants around his neck and stomach contained more than 4,000 pieces of turquoise. When Wetherill picked up a turquoise-trimmed cylindrical basket nearby, he found it surprisingly heavy and was stunned to find upwards of 5,000 turquoise and shell beads and pendants inside.

By the time they stopped work in September, the Hyde team had accumulated enough artifacts for the museum to fill a freight car. Besides pottery, semiprecious stones, and skeletons, there were wooden flutes, stone animal effigies, and scores more of the wooden staffs, which may have been prayer sticks used in ritual observances. Wetherill had also acquired a fiancée—he and 20-year-old Marietta Palmer of the music-making Palmers were married later that year—and a nickname: The Navajos called him Anasazi.

The expedition returned to Pueblo Bonito each of the next three years, eventually uncovering a total of 190 rooms—including several capacious kivas—and running up a $25,000 bill for the deep-pocketed Hydes. The cowboy Richard Wetherill had finally earned his archaeological spurs: He recognized pottery similar to that made by the Mesa Verde people among the deposits at Pueblo Bonito, which indicated to him that the more northerly Anasazi might have moved from their cliff houses to Chaco. Wetherill also found bones of birds identified as macaws, the large parrots found no farther north than tropical Mexico. This discovery showed that there must have been commerce between the Anasazi and the Mexican peoples.

Richard Wetherill's career as an archaeologist ultimately succumbed to a siege mounted by concerned academics and government bureaucrats. Charges of spoliation and profiteering led to an investigation by the government's General Land Office that shut down the Hyde dig in 1900. Wetherill, who had established a home and a trading post at Chaco, was barred from further archaeological work in the canyon, which became a national monument in 1907. Three years later, at the age of 52, he was shot to death following a violent argument between one of his ranch hands and several Navajos over a stolen horse. His bank account showed a balance of $74.23. He was respectfully laid to rest in an Anasazi midden—where they buried their own dead—not 300 yards from the back wall of Pueblo Bonito. Dabney Ford, resident archaeologist at Chaco Culture National Historical Park, has commented that she finds it "altogether fitting that Wetherill lies with his ancient friends."

Subsequent surveys of Chaco by the archaeologists Neil Judd, Frank Roberts, and Gordon Vivian traced the earliest occupation of the canyon by Basket Makers back to between AD 500 and 850, and suggested a peak population of more than 5,000—a figure that would be drastically revised by later excavations. Judd, a young Smithsonian Institution scientist who led a seven-year expedition in the 1920s sponsored by the National Geographic Society, was as wonderstruck by Pueblo Bonito as Lieutenant Simpson and Anasazi Wetherill had been. "No other apartment house of comparable size was known in America or in the Old World," he wrote, "until the Spanish Flats were erected in 1882 at 59th Street and Seventh Avenue, New York City."

Judd's most sublime discovery happened almost by chance in a small interior room where pots, baskets, and parts of skeletons had been found. Acting on impulse, he scraped his trowel over a section of the floor that had already been cleared and struck several beads. Switching to an awl and brush, he kept poking and turned up an "incomparable" four-strand turquoise necklace and two pairs of "marvelously blue" earrings.

"I cannot adequately describe the thrill of that discovery," Judd wrote. "A casual scrape . . . a stroke as mechanical as a thousand

Like a relief map of the thriving community it once was, the ruins of the Hohokam settlement now known as Snaketown stand sharply etched by the harsh light of the Arizona desert. A seven-month-long dig begun in 1964 by a team from the Arizona State Museum laid bare the site's complex pattern of house floors and walls. Dwellings for as many as 500 people were built and rebuilt here over a period of more than 1,000 years starting around the first century AD.

Emil Haury, leader of the 1964-65 excavations at Snaketown, poses inside one of the network of canals the Hohokam dug to divert water to their crops from the Gila River. The first people to irrigate within what is now the continental United States, they apparently used sharpened sticks to gouge out channels, as is indicated by scrape marks still visible in places.

Built around AD 800 and first excavated in 1934, an oval depression 185 feet long and 63 feet wide served as one of Snaketown's ball courts, similar to those found in Mexico. The game, too, was probably patterned after the Mexican version, in which players attempted—using only hips and arms—to pass a ball through hoops set high in the walls.

other strokes made every day, exposed the long-hidden treasure." Word of the find electrified his Zuni and Navajo crewmen, who hurried over to gaze at the spectacular jewelry. The material that had held the necklace together was mostly gone, but Judd managed to preserve the sequence of disks with the aid of a banjo string borrowed from a workman.

One issue that remained unsettled after the early work by Judd's National Geographic expedition was the dates the Anasazi had occupied the "great houses" in Chaco Canyon. They obviously preceded the Spanish arrival in the 16th century, but by how long? The key to the answer came from a scientist whose field was not ancient civilizations but heavenly bodies.

Andrew E. Douglass, an astronomer at the University of Arizona, first began a study of tree rings in 1901 as a means of understanding the relation between sunspots and weather patterns *(page 90)*. Sunspots occur in regular 11-year cycles that, in the Southwest, seem to parallel rainfall levels. Douglass reasoned that tree rings, whose relative thickness from year to year is primarily determined by precipitation, might correspond to sunspot cycles. He was never able to prove this connection, but using timbers from Pueblo Bonito and other southwestern sites, he revolutionized the science of archaeological dating and later fixed the construction of Pueblo Bonito to the period between AD 919 and 1130.

Just as vexing to early southwestern archaeologists were the questions of how many prehistoric cultures had lived in this diverse and demanding land, and what had distinguished them from one another. On the basis of a 1992 discovery, scientists now tentatively identify the original inhabitants of the area as a hunter-gatherer people who left palm prints and fingerprints dating as far back as 28,000 years ago. Evidence of such prints may push the earliest occupation of the Southwest back from the previously accepted date of approximately 9500 BC, which itself had derived from radiocarbon dating of chipped stone points that had been discovered near the New Mexico town of Clovis. The Clovis points were embedded in the ribs of a species of mammoth that disappeared during the last Ice Age.

By about 6000 BC—the beginning of the Archaic Period—these hunter-gatherers had evolved into a somewhat more sedentary foraging and small-game-hunting folk. These were the ancestors of the Anasazi, who emerged around AD 200 and dominated the early archaeological agenda because of the fascination engendered by the cliff dwellings and by Chaco Canyon. But even in Wetherill's day, there were those who sensed different rhythms and styles, and suspected that the Southwest was never an exclusively Anasazi province.

Frank Hamilton Cushing was a New Yorker so infatuated with southwestern Indians that he spent four years living and working at the Zuni pueblo in the 1880s and 15 months more excavating a curious cluster of mounds in Arizona's Salt River valley as a Smithsonian anthropologist. The results of Cushing's work did not appear in print until more than 50 years later, but he was nevertheless the first to explore the culture later identified as Hohokam, a Pima word that translates as "ancestors" or "used-up people."

The Hohokam, who lived in the Salt and Gila valleys in the region embracing the modern cities of Phoenix and Tucson, came into focus through the work of Harold Gladwin, a stockbroker turned amateur archaeologist, and Emil Haury, the former head of the University of Arizona's anthropology department and the dean of contemporary southwestern archaeology. Gladwin dated his scientific awakening to a 1924 outing with the respected Harvard scholar Alfred V. Kidder, during which they passed an unexplored ruin. They stopped at the site, Gladwin wrote, and "by the time we had made a collection my future course was set."

Cushing, Kidder, and others over the decades had seen in the desert dwellers a different culture, and Haury and Gladwin confirmed their suppositions during a multiyear study of the site of Snaketown, in the Phoenix Basin. Hohokam red-on-buff pottery was unlike anything the Anasazi made. The Hohokam cremated their dead and lived not in apartment-style pueblos but in detached rectangular one-room houses. They also built a vast network of irrigation canals, constructed ball courts as some Mesoamerican peoples did, and crafted a unique array of shell jewelry, clay figurines, and stone objects. There was some initial skepticism toward the acceptance of another prehistoric desert culture—one academic remarked to Haury that they were not Hohokam but hokum. By 1931, however, most of the doubts had subsided.

Five years later, Haury was also responsible for the identification of the Mogollon of the New Mexico-Arizona mountains as another distinct entity. The Mogollon were originally thought to be a regional variant of the Anasazi because of similarities in their pueblos and pottery, but further research demonstrated that this was the result of their two separate cultural traditions having coalesced. Haury, who excavated the first villages definitively classified as Mogollon, showed that before AD 1000 Mogollon houses and pottery were distinctive and that the mountain-based Mogollon stressed hunting far more than did the Anasazi or the Hohokam. Other archaeologists found in the captivating Mimbres pottery fashioned by a Mogollon subgroup an artwork as singular as it was handsome.

Some of the black-on-white Mimbres bowls depict humans, animals, fish, insects, and mythical creatures in an imaginative style, but most display symmetrical, balanced, perfectly executed geometric designs. Their creators lived in a cluster of villages along the Mimbres River in southwestern New Mexico between the 11th and 13th centuries. The amateur archaeologists Cornelius and Harriet Cosgrove of Silver City, New Mexico, led the first systematic recovery of Mimbres bowls at a site called Swarts Ruin in the 1920s, even before the Mogollon were recognized as a distinct culture. The Cosgroves found 635 pots placed as burial offerings with bodies interred beneath hard-packed adobe floors. Holes punched in the bowls may have signified a ritualistic "killing" that apparently accompanied burial.

Like all Southwest artists, the Mimbres potters worked with brushes made from the fiber of yucca leaves shredded at one end to form bristles. Their touch was so delicate that they could paint as many as 15 parallel lines in a border just three-fourths of an inch wide. The leading characters in the pottery stories were often figures still prominent in the myths of present-day southwestern Indians: the Humpbacked Flute Player, who symbolizes fertility and reproduction, and Spider Woman, the earth mother.

"Mimbres ceramic decoration has an archaeological value beyond the aesthetic," according to the archaeologist Stephen Lekson. "Mimbres art depicts plants, people, insects, and animals with great accuracy and detail." The art historian J. J. Brody of the University of New Mexico describes the spiritual world revealed in Mimbres art as a universe "kept harmonious by the careful and rigid balancing of all conceivable oppositions."

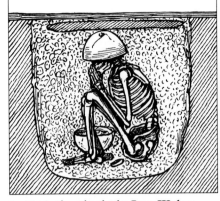

In 1914, the ethnologist Jesse Walter Fewkes investigated a remarkable find in the Mimbres area of southwestern New Mexico. Hundreds of bowls, intricately painted, had been unearthed. The drawing above, from his subsequent report, indicates that some bowls were interred with the dead. Fewkes's illustrations (below) *show just a few of the thousands of geometric designs painted on Mimbres pottery.*

POTTERY BY DESIGN: THE MIMBRES STORY

If their pottery is any indication, the ancient peoples who lived along the Mimbres River valley in southwestern New Mexico developed an increasing appreciation for the artistic side of life. Early examples of their work, dating to the third century AD, bear no decoration and served primarily as cooking and storage vessels. But by the 11th century, glorious new styles had emerged, with the finest pieces apparently reserved for ceremonial uses. Bowls were often buried with the dead and were sometimes placed over the corpse's head, their painted scenes affording the departed a last view from the world of the living.

Mimbres potters painted their wares with a mixture of powdered hematite, clay, and water; color variations owe to differences in the firing temperature and the richness of oxygen in the kiln. The designs themselves have had an enduring appeal—prized so highly by collectors that in the 1960s some looters bulldozed sites in search of buried troves.

The figures on the Mimbres bowl above may depict a myth picked up and told by post-European-contact Indians, in which the Hero Twins draw rain from the mouth of a monster known as Cloud Swallower, thereby ending a drought. The hole punched in its center—a ritual gesture thought by some scholars to represent the freeing of the object's indwelling spirit—marks this as a funerary bowl.

Mimbres designs range from abstract patterns, as on the bowl at right, to representational depictions of animals, such as the bighorn-sheep jar shown below. Effigy jars like this one may have been used for storing seeds over the winter in preparation for the spring planting.

Flying insects swarm around the interior of this small, six-inch-wide bowl. An oxygen-rich kiln atmosphere produced the reddish hue; less oxygen would have yielded a darker shade or black.

With the look of modern art, the stylized renderings of mountain sheep above and a lizard at left are typical of the designs that have proved so attractive to 20th-century art collectors.

The earliest Mogollon, dating back to about AD 200, lived in half-buried pit houses roofed with saplings and reeds. They subsisted primarily on wild game supplemented with corn, beans, squash, nuts, and seeds. Their villages, mainly in the mountains but also in adjoining valleys, were groups of houses arranged in no particular plan or pattern. They built kivas and ceremonial structures as the Anasazi did, but theirs were usually rectangular rather than round.

Artifacts from New Mexico's Tularosa Cave indicate that the Mogollon wore fur-and-feather robes, played reed flutes, smoked tobacco in tubular pipes (probably only on special occasions), and gambled with dicelike pieces—some pottery scenes portray abashed losers. In areas where game was elusive they suffered from the effects of a low-protein diet. Skeletons at one late Mogollon ruin showed evidence of bone lesions caused by both anemia and infections.

The archaeologist Steven LeBlanc concluded from his work at Mogollon villages in the 1970s that their society was essentially egalitarian, with no sign of class distinctions. There were no sumptuous burials, no house grander than any other, no caches of luxury goods like those at Pueblo Bonito. Despite the excellence of the Mimbres pottery, there was no evidence of craft specialization. Nor

The Gila Cliff Dwellings fill five caverns 180 feet above a creek bed high in southwestern New Mexico's Mogollon Mountains, for which the people that built these masonry structures late in the 13th century AD were named. The well-concealed main entrance (above), *reached by a vertigo-inducing ascent, provided security from intruders. Natural archways in the rock* (opposite) *interconnect the three easternmost caves.*

was any one village more imposing than the others. According to LeBlanc, "there is little evidence of actual trade or of the movement of people" before they came under Anasazi influence.

Some Mogollon men apparently belonged to groups anthropologists call sodalities, associations often symbolized by particular ornaments found with skeletons. Shell pendants, bone hairpins, and arrowhead clusters may have signified three such "lodges" at an eastern Arizona site on Grasshopper Plateau, but their exact meaning and function remain unknown. A late 1970s study of burial practices at Grasshopper reported by the archaeologist J. Jefferson Reid of the University of Arizona showed that children up to age nine were generally buried without artifacts, but that thereafter the number of grave objects interred with them increased until they reached what he interpreted as adulthood at the age of 15.

The conventional wisdom for 50 years was that the Mogollon were considerably less sophisticated than the Hohokam or the Anasazi, and that they had a genius for pottery but few other distinctions. Their villages in particular were derided as slapdash in comparison with the Anasazi cliff dwellings at Mesa Verde until tree-ring dating in the 1970s revealed that they were not contemporary at all: The

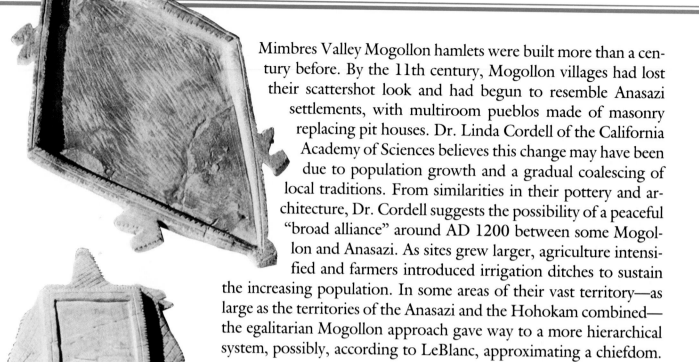

A pair of stone palettes, used as surfaces for grinding and mixing face and body paints primarily used in cremation rites, attest to the artistry of Hohokam culture. Designs ranged from the relatively plain example at top to more elaborately ornamented pieces, such as the six-inch-long representation of a horned toad above. Palettes have turned up most often in burial grounds.

Mimbres Valley Mogollon hamlets were built more than a century before. By the 11th century, Mogollon villages had lost their scattershot look and had begun to resemble Anasazi settlements, with multiroom pueblos made of masonry replacing pit houses. Dr. Linda Cordell of the California Academy of Sciences believes this change may have been due to population growth and a gradual coalescing of local traditions. From similarities in their pottery and architecture, Dr. Cordell suggests the possibility of a peaceful "broad alliance" around AD 1200 between some Mogollon and Anasazi. As sites grew larger, agriculture intensified and farmers introduced irrigation ditches to sustain the increasing population. In some areas of their vast territory—as large as the territories of the Anasazi and the Hohokam combined—the egalitarian Mogollon approach gave way to a more hierarchical system, possibly, according to LeBlanc, approximating a chiefdom.

The Hohokam people who lived a few hundred miles away on the cactus-spiked desert of south central Arizona managed the remarkable feat of building and maintaining a culture based on irrigation agriculture that endured for more than a millennium. In a parched landscape, the Hohokam scattered their settlements along rare streams and shallow wells, and they built the most sophisticated prehistoric irrigation system north of Mexico. Archaeologists, working with a scant supply of datable trees, disagree on how long the Hohokam survived on nature's skimpy blessings, but the current consensus estimates their cultural lifespan at more than 1,100 years, from about AD 200 to 1450.

The details of their extensive irrigation network—more than 400 miles of canals in the Phoenix area alone, some recognized with the aid of satellite imagery—illustrate the complexity of Hohokam engineering and their environmental savvy. The canals were deep and narrow—as much as seven feet deep and only six to 10 feet wide—which meant less surface area exposed to sunlight and thus less evaporation. Ditches and diversion channels bore water from the Salt and Gila rivers to fields where farmers grew corn, squash, beans, cotton, pumpkins, and other crops, possibly harvesting twice a year. Ironically, flooding from these same life-giving rivers may have damaged or destroyed some of the unlined canals.

In the early 1980s, the archaeologists Paul and Suzanne Fish

Among the most exquisitely crafted of Hohokam artifacts, shells dating from around AD 1000 offer proof that this southwestern culture was the world's first to develop etching. Designs were drawn in pitch, and then a mildly acidic liquid, probably fermented saguaro-cactus juice, was applied to eat away exposed surfaces.

Carved from glycymeris shell, most likely from the Gulf of California, this bracelet reflects the Hohokam interest in snakes. Archaeologist Emil Haury was "baffled by the incredible finesse of the working of" such artifacts, which have been found in connection with cremations.

wondered how much labor it took to build the Hohokam canals and devised a formula to find out. They calculated that no more than about 200 miles of the total canal system would have been functional at any one time. From this they extracted a figure for the volume of earth that had to be moved—1,179,000 cubic yards. Using World Health Organization numbers as a guideline, they estimated that one laborer could have moved 1.31 cubic yards a day. This gave them an answer: A hundred men working a month a year would have needed 420 years to build the main canal network; laboring three months a year, it would have taken them 140 years. But more questions remained: How many diggers were actually involved, and how long did the whole project take? Was the labor voluntary or compulsory? Who was in charge?

Hohokam builders did not stop with canals. Some 200 ball courts—sunken oval fields on which a ceremonial ball game was presumably played—have been identified at Hohokam sites. In the Phoenix Basin, five ball courts were built at settlements about four miles apart. The game probably resembled one played in Mexico in which players moved a rubber ball—without using their hands or feet—down a rectangular field and tried to get it through a stone ring high on a wall. At the Snaketown site, one field was 185 feet long and 63 feet wide with earthen banks along either side. Three stone markers were found, one at each end and another midway between them, but no rings. Also found at the site were effigies of what appear to be ballplayers, showing them wearing shin and shoulder pads.

The ball courts exemplify an issue that continues to divide archaeologists: whether the Hohokam originated in Mexico or evolved from indigenous southwestern roots. Ceremonial and luxury artifacts made in Mesoamerica, such as copper bells and mosaic pyrite mirrors, have been found at Hohokam sites, as have macaw bones. Some

researchers have argued that Hohokam cultural traits resemble those of the Mexican cultures more than they do those of the Archaic cultures that preceded them (though Gladwin allowed that his conviction was "more obstinate than scientific"). But most modern scholars think that all southwestern Indians derive from the Archaic tribes. And there, for the moment at least, the matter rests.

A Hohokam village was a series of pole-walled, grass-roofed mud houses sometimes arranged in clusters of two to six that might have been family groups. The people ate corn in a variety of ways as well as squash, an assortment of beans, various desert plants, and sometimes venison or rabbit. The stones they used for grinding corn left deposits of grit that took a toll on their teeth. A study of skeletons found at a late site in Phoenix showed that the Hohokam, like their contemporaries, suffered from gum disease. Many had arthritis, and older women often exhibited signs of osteoporosis. By analyzing bones and extrapolating information about the attached muscles, scholars learned that men frequently had strong upper arms, pre-

The Hohokam ruins of Casa Grande—Big House—rise 35 feet above Arizona's Sonoran Desert. Built around AD 1300, the multistory structure may have functioned as residence, administrative center, storehouse, and observatory. Its adobe walls were made of a lime-rich subsoil; a modern shelter wards off further erosion.

104

sumably due to the manual labor they performed, and women had well-developed hands, possibly from grinding corn. The human figurines they molded out of clay offer another clue to their appearance, suggesting that they wrapped their hair in headbands and turbans, wore earrings and cheek plugs, and favored body paint or tattoos.

The Hohokam were fond of jewelry and produced a stunning variety of rings, bracelets, pendants, hairpins, cheek and lip plugs, and other pieces fashioned from turquoise, jet, and shells from the Gulf of California. They developed an etching technique that at the time was unique in the world. The etcher first used pitch to draw a design on a shell, then dipped the shell into a weak acid—probably fermented cactus juice—that ate away the uncovered parts and left the design standing out in relief. Haury conducted successful experiments with this technique, using a potion made from saguaro cactus.

Archaeologists are still trying to fathom Hohokam society. Were there chiefs or shamans? Haury thought so. A skeleton found at the Casa Buena site in Phoenix was taller than average, showed no evidence of physical labor, and was buried near a kit holding bone awls, a bracelet, and a variety of minerals. Some burial and cremation sites (the Hohokam used both methods) contain shell jewelry and other luxury goods—perhaps indicating that the dead had been aristocrats. The archaeologist Jill Neitzel found materials used in ceramic manufacture in only a few houses at Snaketown, implying that these were the workshops of full-time artisans. Specialization like that presumes organization, a chain of command; but, in the absence of written records, the details of how it functioned still perplex scholars.

Platform mounds—elevated sites found at prominent locations in some late Hohokam villages and along canal routes—seem to have been used as ceremonial centers and as walled-off "great houses" where the elite lived. Clearly, all Hohokam were not equal. But how the canals were built and how farmland was allocated remain puzzles.

In the last phase of the Hohokam chronicle there are signs of a mingling with other cultures. Different types of pottery appear, including a very few Mimbres bowls. Gladwin speculated that the Hohokam kidnapped Mogollon women, but there is no evidence of warfare in the long Hohokam record. Housing changed from single-story compounds to Anasazi-like pueblos. Village walls appeared, suggesting a need for defense or privacy. Where cremation had previously been practiced by most people, bodies were now also buried.

Still another enigma lingers in the Hohokam shadows. In a

large building at Casa Grande, Arizona, the two edges of an upper-story round window line up precisely with the setting sun on the summer solstice each year. All the agricultural peoples of the Southwest had some sort of calendar system, but the details of their astronomical knowledge—such as whether they used this and other structures as observatories—remain obscure.

Perhaps the most mystifying of all the ancient southwestern cultures was that of the Sinagua, the people "without water," who built timber-lined pit houses and grew corn in the high, dry country east of Flagstaff, Arizona. In their peak years, from about AD 1125 to 1215, the Sinagua may have been a conduit for the exchange of goods and ideas—a veritable melting pot for the assorted southwestern peoples. Sometime in the 13th century, they moved south to the fertile Verde Valley, where they stayed for another 200 years. Why they departed remains a mystery, but their later sites are recognized as ancestral by the Hopi.

The Fremont people, named for the Fremont River in eastern Utah, were an enterprising group who scattered small rock-and-adobe granaries around their rugged domain. For archaeologists, the foremost riddle about the Fremont is where they came from. When they were first identified and described in 1931, investigators postulated that they had split off from the Anasazi, but the many differences between the two cultures make this doubtful. Others have suggested that the Fremont evolved from the Archaic people—an unlikely possibility, given the time lag between them. A third theory, that they derived from a high-plains people who migrated south, suffers from a shortage of evidence.

The Fremont ranged through eastern Utah and the northwestern corner of Colorado between about AD 700 and 1300, sustaining themselves with hunting and farming. Their tiny granaries, often hidden beneath rock ledges or atop steep cliffs, had small openings that helped spawn a legend of two-foot-high folk dwelling in miniature stone huts. They also built larger rock towers—probably for food storage as well—and placed them at easily defended sites, suggesting a vigilant stance against real or supposed enemies. In their villages, the Fremont lived in a variety of dwellings including pit houses with saucer-shaped floors, but they also maintained throughout their territory what appears to be a network of shelters where

Appearing to grow right out of the sheer rockface, the cliff-dwelling community known as Palatki—Hopi for "red house"—is among the largest and best-preserved ruins in central Arizona's Red Rocks region. Between AD 1100 and 1300 it was home to as many as 50 members of the mysterious Sinagua culture.

wayfarers could pass the night.

They survive most vividly in elaborate pictographs showing animals, plants, and people with triangular or trapezoidal bodies, often decked out in headdresses and necklaces. They also emerge as individualists in the gray pottery they created in a tremendous variety of forms—sleek and rotund, flared and flat-edged, with and without handles, animal-shaped and narrow-mouthed.

One by one these societies of the ancient Southwest had risen. They made their enduring mark—on the earth itself and in their intriguing use of its raw materials—then moved on, abandoning their great pueblos and cliff houses, their canals and sheltering valleys. Chaco Canyon, grandest of them all, was finally empty by 1300, its fine stone pueblos already sinking beneath wind-driven sand. Mesa Verde, too, was deserted by 1300, the Fremont villages by about the same time. The Mogollon settlements in the Mimbres Valley had become ghost towns a century earlier, followed about a generation afterward by the Sinagua settlements in Verde Valley. Last to go from their ancestral homeland were the Hohokam, the canal builders and ballplayers and etchers; by 1450 their culture in the Salt and Gila valleys had flickered out.

The exodus of these peoples, both individually and collectively, is the great and enduring drama of the prehistoric Southwest. Drought, war, flood, famine, plague—all these and more have been offered as explanations that have been debated, qualified, combined, and ultimately rejected. Because the archaeological record halts with the end of the settlements, researchers can only grope for answers, and theories flourish in the absence of strong evidence.

Tree-ring analysis documents a major drought in Anasazi country between 1276 and 1299. Did crop failures, vanishing game, and a lack of water drive the Cliff Dwellers from Mesa Verde? The archaeologist Linda Cordell, who has meticulously examined the various abandonment theories, thinks not. She cites data showing that some sites were built during those years. The Anasazi had survived drought before; there was no discernible reason why this one would have triggered an exodus.

The warfare theory likewise withers under Cordell's scrutiny. Harold Gladwin was among those who espoused the notion of a violent disruption, blaming the ancestors of the Navajos and Apaches. "In every village in the Southwest at AD 1200," he wrote, "the same questions are being asked: Where to go? What to do to obtain relief from the ceaseless persecution of marauding Athabascans?" Cordell notes, however, that the Athabascans did not arrive until about 1500—too late to do any harm—and that evidence supporting the specter of large-scale violence is largely absent.

Did an epidemic, perhaps imported from the tropics, wipe them out? The pueblos were at their largest and most populous not long before their demise, conditions hospitable to the spread of disease. But no large burial concentrations have been found. Experts on the Hohokam cite data showing that flash floods may have ravaged their canals in the late 14th century, but the desert dwellers persisted for more than 50 years afterward.

Some scientists believe that "ecological suicide"—the destruction of their environment—brought the great centers of these ancient southwestern peoples down. In this reckoning, they felled too many trees in their sparse forests, destroyed the watersheds, and their crops failed. Cordell supports a related view: Populations increased, rainfall decreased, the pressures to move mounted, and families packed up and left—not suddenly or in large groups, but slowly and steadily.

In fact, the prehistoric peoples did not vanish at all; they became the nucleus of present-day tribes such as the Rio Grande Pueblo, Zuni, Hopi, Pima, and Papago. To consider them lost cultures, as the archaeologist Gary Matlock writes of the Anasazi, "is roughly comparable to viewing those who left England for the New World as having mysteriously disappeared." Transformed by new experiences and new surroundings, they survived, even as the details of their former lives faded away.

THE SAGA OF "GREEN TABLE"

The Anasazi who established their homes in the caves and cliffs of Mesa Verde had been gone for more than 450 years when the first Spanish traders reached this remote and forbidding quarter of the West in the 18th century. But the journals left by one of their number in 1765 and by two Franciscan friars 11 years later say nothing at all about the mesa or the intricate, multitiered cliff dwellings.

Mesa Verde—Spanish for "green table"—had been so named for the dense piñon and juniper forests on its flat summit even before the priests passed by en route to California. In 1829 a Spanish expedition penetrated the Mancos Valley on the edge of the mesa, but it, too, missed the ruins, an understandable failure considering their location in the most distant reaches of the canyons that cut deeply into the mesa's bulk. The presence of hostile Ute Indians made detailed exploration of the mesa a risky venture, though the Utes themselves shunned the cliff houses and their ghosts.

In 1859 Dr. John Newberry, a geologist with the San Juan Exploring Expedition, became the first outsider to climb the mesa's daunting wall; but Newberry, too, failed to see the cliff houses and was not much impressed with the landscape he beheld. "To us as well as to all the civilized world, it was a terra incognita," he wrote dismissively. But while a systematic study of the Anasazi by men like those scrambling intrepidly up a cliff in the photograph at center was still some years away, Mesa Verde and its wonders would not remain incognita much longer.

Photographer Jackson (left) temporarily yielded the camera to another member of his party for this picture of the New Yorker-turned-Westerner en route to the Mesa Verde cliff dwellings.

EXPLORING WITH A CAMERA

In the summer of 1874, William Henry Jackson, a gifted photographer and a member of the Hayden Survey mapping the Rocky Mountains, met an old friend on the trail in southwestern Colorado. He told Jackson tales of fabulous cliff houses at Mesa Verde, stories he had heard from a miner named John Moss, who had made his own peace with the truculent Utes. The excited Jackson, accompanied by the reporter Ernest Ingersoll and their packers, immediately set off in search of Moss and the ruins.

The miner agreed to guide them to the cliff dwellings, and, in return, Jackson's party did him a small favor—Moss needed their votes in his campaign for office in the mining camp of Parrott City (population about a dozen), where residency requirements were conveniently loose. Jackson and Ingersoll cast their ballots, Moss was elected, and they headed off to Mesa Verde.

The next day, Jackson's men muscled his heavy camera and 5-by-8-inch glass plates up a 700-foot cliff—negotiating the final 50 feet with the help of ancient handholds and footholds cut in the stone—so he could take these photographs, including the background picture showing Moss *(standing)* and Ingersoll at the site Jackson named Two-Story Cliff House. It was "worth everything I possessed," Jackson later wrote. He then moved on in search of other sites, finding a few but missing the spectacular houses in the side canyons.

The published descriptions by Jackson and Ingersoll sparked the first scientific interest in Mesa Verde and even an exhibit at the 1876 Centennial Exposition in Philadelphia, but it would take one more discovery to snare the public's imagination.

William Henry Jackson and company assembled in Parrott City for this picture, with the photographer third from left. The others (left to right) *are guide-interpreter Harry Lee, packer Bob Mitchell, a naturalist named Barber, an unidentified packer, and Charlie the cook. Lee, who spoke the Ute language, took over as guide when John Moss was called to San Francisco on business.*

IN PURSUIT OF WEALTH AND KNOWLEDGE

The 1888 discovery of Cliff Palace by Richard Wetherill transformed Mesa Verde from a scientific curiosity into a major tourist attraction. Richard spent the next two winters mining the cliff dwellings for salable relics; his ranch filled up with axes and yucca-leaf sandals in addition to crateloads of pottery.

Following mixed reviews from local audiences, he took his road show to Denver and included a new discovery, the mummy of an infant. The display became an overnight sensation, and he sold the collection to the Colorado Historical Society for $3,000.

The Wetherill family's willingness to turn a profit from the artifacts they amassed changed forever with the 1891 arrival of the young Swedish aristocrat Gustav Nordenskiöld, who had seen the exhibit in Denver. He spent the summer at Mesa Verde introducing them to scientific methods, teaching them to use trowels and whisk brooms and to catalog their finds.

As Nordenskiöld prepared to leave, a group of Durango citizens sued to stop him from freighting his large relic collection to Europe, but the case was dismissed. Back home, he authored the first major book about Mesa Verde prehistory before he died of tuberculosis at 26.

Two of the five Wetherill brothers, John (left) and Richard, take a lunch break while sorting through artifacts at Spruce Tree House. Richard discovered the ruin (named for a tree growing through an outer wall) on the same December day that he and his brother-in-law Charlie Mason first spied the Cliff Palace ruin.

Gustav Nordenskiöld (left), whose photo appears against a background image of Cliff Palace in 1891, came to the Southwest in hopes of alleviating his tuberculosis. His father had been a noted Arctic explorer and mineralogist. The young Swede was scientifically trained but not an archaeologist. Fascinated by the ruins, he sent home for his camera and spent the entire summer at Mesa Verde.

Groups of tourists like this hardy crew rode horseback to Mesa Verde on the canyonside Crinkley Edge Trail. Guide Richard Wetherill (third from right) and his brothers advised visitors that they need not fear "danger or discomfort," though one woman complained that the water at the Wetherills' Alamo Ranch was so alkaline that it "takes off what little skin the piñons leave." This 1889 party included the Sumners, a distinguished Washington, D.C., family.

CRUSADERS FOR PROTECTION

The tourist boom at Mesa Verde began in earnest after 12 million visitors to the 1893 Columbian Exposition in Chicago viewed an exhibit of scale models of cliff houses. The enterprising Wetherills transformed their home into a dude ranch, offering room and board for two dollars a day and guided trips to the ruins for five dollars. One visitor recalled that guides would sometimes detonate dynamite charges to rout rattlesnakes before leading people into the ruins. By the mid-1890s Sunday outings devoted to pot hunting had become a popular pastime.

In the absence of protective laws, visitors were free to pillage at will; and many took full advantage of the opportunity, assembling caches of skulls, pottery, and other artifacts like the 1904 haul shown in the background photograph. Proposals for protection of the site that had begun as early as 1889 grew more insistent in the late 1890s. In 1906, a campaign of more than a decade led by a pair of extraordinary women *(below)* resulted in the creation of the first national park celebrating the achievements of a prehistoric culture.

When she first visited Mesa Verde as a newspaper correspondent in 1882, Virginia McClurg (above) traveled atop a vinegar barrel in a freighter's wagon. A dozen years later, as a teacher and poet, she led the drive to preserve the cliff dwellings. McClurg and her deputy, Lucy Peabody (above, right) made speeches illustrated with newfangled stereopticon views and organized VIP tours of the sites. They lobbied legislators, negotiated a lease with the Utes, and won the backing of the 250,000-strong Federation of Women's Clubs. Both sensed that the U.S. Congress offered their plan a better chance of success than the Colorado legislature. On the brink of victory in 1906, however, McClurg suddenly split their group into bitter factions by reverting to the idea of a state park—which she would have controlled—but Peabody and the national park prevailed.

PRESERVATION AND SKILLFUL RESTORATION

The first task for the new federal managers at Mesa Verde was undoing the damage that two decades of unimpeded vandalism had wrought. Pot hunters had left many cliff houses stripped of their treasures and littered with rubble (as can be seen in the background picture of Mug House).

The Smithsonian archaeologist Jesse Fewkes directed the cleanup at Spruce Tree House and Cliff Palace in 1908-9 and at 14 more sites in the ensuing decade. Many of the ruins' walls were reinforced or stabilized to prevent further deterioration. Fewkes, who aspired to make "the mystical red man" known to the general public, introduced the first campfire talks given at a national park.

The archaeologist Jesse Nusbaum, who became park superintendent in 1921, continued the stabilization work and pressed successfully for an end to cattle grazing in the park. Nusbaum also welcomed an especially notable visitor in 1921—the photographer William Henry Jackson, now 78, who had climbed the canyon wall nearly a half-century earlier.

Laborers using horse-drawn machinery (below) unearth masonry walls at a mesa-top site called Far View House in 1916. Archaeologists believe that the mesa sites antedated the cliff dwellings, which were inhabited for only about a hundred years. Excavations led by archaeologists Jesse Fewkes (who took this picture) and Jesse Nusbaum after the U.S. Congress declared Mesa Verde a national park discovered artifacts from several layers of settlement, confirming that some mesa-top villages had been occupied repeatedly.

Jesse Fewkes (below) *had spent 20 years exploring archaeological sites in the Southwest before he came to Mesa Verde in 1908. In this photograph taken a decade later, he stands in front of the converted ranger station that became Mesa Verde's—and the Park Service's—first museum. Tourist amenities at the park were still crude enough in those years that a pamphlet distributed to visitors warned of sharp turns and frequent washouts on the main access road.*

A RENOWNED PHOTOGRAPHER'S TRIBUTE

By October 1941, when the legendary photographer Ansel Adams came to Mesa Verde, he beheld a fully realized national park. The massive stabilization projects had been completed. Under the Emergency Works Program of the federal government, the Civilian Conservation Corps (CCC) had brought park services up to speed by constructing roads, cabins, trails, and campgrounds. The number of visitors, which had multiplied sixfold during the 1920s, was rapidly approaching 17,000 a year.

Adams, who had been photographing Yosemite Park for two decades, was invited by Interior Secretary Harold Ickes to tour the national parks to create a set of murals for a Department of the Interior museum—"one of the best ideas ever to come out of Washington," Adams called it. (His $22.22 daily wage was the top rate paid government consultants at the time.)

Adams worked his customary magic at Mesa Verde (as is shown by the pictures on these pages), but the outbreak of World War II forced the abandonment of the mural project soon afterward, despite the photographer's argument that his pictures were in fact "an emotional presentation of what we are fighting for."

Ansel Adams, shown here on top of his station wagon, was 39 when he visited Mesa Verde and already celebrated for his nature photography. The 225 prints he sent to Washington after his tour of the national parks lay forgotten for years following the cancellation of the mural project. Adams died in 1984.

Adams's hauntingly beautiful images of the Watch Tower (left) and Cliff Palace (opposite) convey the sense of awe and mystery that motivated generations of farsighted conservationists to protect these irreplaceable national treasures.

THE ANASAZI: MASTERS OF THE CANYONS AND CLIFFS

The afternoon sun illuminates Window Arch, one of the many spectacular natural features of Canyon de Chelly, Arizona. The Anasazi made their home here for more than a thousand years.

Adolph Bandelier personified the blend of adventurous spirit and scientific inquisitiveness that marked the 19th century and produced a bevy of distinguished explorers. Alexander von Humboldt, Richard Burton, and David Livingstone, among others, had taken new scientific theories and methodologies and set out for the world's remaining wild places to test their applicability. In 1880, New Mexico was just such a wild place, and Bandelier, a 40-year-old Swiss immigrant working in his father's Illinois bank, found himself inexorably drawn by the area's frontier mystique.

He whetted his insatiable curiosity by reading everything he could lay his hands on. The accounts of Humboldt, who had explored the impenetrable Amazon, especially stirred him. Bandelier became fascinated with Indians and their culture. Though he grew up in southern Illinois practically in the shadow of Cahokia, the Mound Builders held no interest for him: Others were already studying them. His overriding passion was the unexplored Southwest.

Constantly seeking more knowledge, the banker brashly started writing letters to the leading anthropologists and sociologists of his day. At least one, the eminent Lewis Henry Morgan, author of the highly regarded work *Ancient Society,* responded, beginning a relationship that would shape the rest of Bandelier's life. Morgan, impressed by Bandelier's linguistic ability, discipline, and enthusiasm, used his status to pull strings with the newly formed Archaeological Institute of America (AIA). He obtained financial sponsorship for the two of them to go to the Southwest. The staid Bandelier excitedly wrote to his newfound mentor: "Great, wow, I've arranged my business affairs so we can go. What kind of clothes shall I bring? What kind of gun shall I buy?" Meanwhile, in his methodical Swiss way of preparation, he learned archaic Spanish in order to read the accounts of the conquistadors.

Morgan had to withdraw at the last minute, so Bandelier, with a $1,200-a-year grant from the AIA, made the trip alone. He arrived in Santa Fe, New Mexico, in August 1880, flushed with an awareness that his "life's work has at last begun." Right away he set out for the abandoned pueblo of Pecos, where he spent 10 hectic days measuring ruins and amassing a collection of chipped stone tools, potsherds, rocks, and even bits of adobe mortar. Returning to Santa Fe, he bundled up his haul, drafted a 95-page report, and sent it all back to the AIA, where his manuscript on Pecos became the fledgling institute's first publication.

Unfortunately, his next foray—this time to an active, very conservative pueblo—was not a success. In Santa Fe, a Catholic priest encouraged him to visit nearby Santo Domingo. Ignorant of Pueblo Indian ways, Bandelier immediately upon his arrival began asking probing questions of these gracious, yet secretive, pueblo dwellers. Theirs was a closed society, and they placed legitimate restrictions on the movements and activities of their guest, constraints that were anathema to a driven man like Bandelier. Once, he was cautioned not to attend a funeral but proceeded to spy on the ceremony from an open window. After several such breaches of etiquette, the pueblo's leaders at last became fed up with the overbearing outsider and asked him to leave. Bandelier dug in his heels and refused. The response was typical of this nonviolent people: They cut off his food supply. Chastened, he finally withdrew, to everyone's relief.

Having learned a hard lesson in common courtesy and public relations, Bandelier enjoyed better fortune at his next stop, the Cochiti pueblo southwest of Santa Fe. Apparently he won the leaders' confidence, for they asked him to serve as recorder for the tribal court. During his stay, he hired a Cochiti guide, Juan José Montoya, to take him through the surrounding mesas and canyons.

In the course of their tour of this rugged country, Montoya

A ruined pueblo abuts the northern wall of Frijoles Canyon in Bandelier National Monument, New Mexico. Additional rooms were carved directly into the soft volcanic rock of the cliff face. A resourceful Anasazi potter repaired the artfully designed vessel at right by tying fiber or sinew through mend holes in the rim.

casually inquired if Bandelier would like to see where the Cochiti used to live. Bandelier readily agreed and, on October 23, 1880, Montoya led him into a canyon called Rito de Frijoles (Spanish for "Bean Creek"). Bandelier was awe-struck by both the scenery and the extensive ruins—including man-made caves—calling them "the grandest thing I ever saw." There, rising before them, were towering cliffs. Along the bottom of one, for an undetermined length, ran abandoned dwellings. Bandelier found the volcanic rock from which these had been carved "so soft that in many places it can be scooped out or detached with the most primitive tools, or even with the fingers alone."

To Bandelier, the canyon's northern cliff face resembled "a huge, irregular honeycomb." The caves, he wrote, "are met with in clusters of as many as several hundred; more frequently, however, the groups are small. Sometimes two or more tiers of caves are superimposed." Upon closer examination, Bandelier noticed many similarities between this abandoned site and the active, Cochiti pueblo. "From the objects scattered about and in the cells, and from the size and disposition of the latter, it becomes evident that the people who excavated and inhabited them were on the same level of culture as the so-called Pueblo Indians of New Mexico."

What the Cochiti guide reverently regarded as his people's old neighborhood was, in fact, one of the truly spectacular and lasting achievements of the Anasazi culture. While other centers of Anasazi life, such as Chaco Canyon and Mesa Verde, withered in the 12th and 13th centuries from a combination of drought and environmental degradation, the caves and pueblos in and around Frijoles Canyon remained viable and even attracted newcomers.

Bandelier, the banker turned scientist, had made a remarkable find. He spent the next few days sketching and measuring the ruins in accordance with his mandate from the AIA, but never undertook a systematic excavation. Smitten with unquenchable wanderlust, Bandelier returned to Frijoles Canyon only four more times. During a total of 18 months in New Mexico, he logged 166 other ruins,

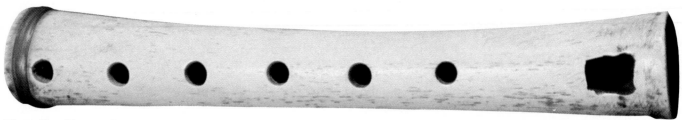

Flutes like this one of carved animal bone are found at excavated pueblos. A legendary flute player, called Kokopelli by modern Hopi Indians of the region, is often portrayed in southwestern rock art as a hunchback or carrying a burden.

then moved on to South America, where he spent 11 years. But in all that time he rarely stayed more than two weeks at any one site. Nevertheless, his discovery on that October day would win him immortality. Two years after Bandelier's death in March of 1914, President Woodrow Wilson signed a bill intended to protect the ruins of the Frijoles Canyon area. Today the 27,000-acre reserve bears the name Bandelier National Monument.

The Anasazi settlement first scouted by Bandelier is an exception to the general conditions under which this hardy people lived. Well watered by Frijoles Creek and the nearby Rio Grande, with forests covering the abutting Jemez Mountains and plenty of mineral-rich volcanic soil, the area stands in stark contrast to the terrain where most Anasazi dwelled. The Four Corners region is predominantly high desert—even its lowlands are mostly above 5,000 feet—where temperatures range from 100 degrees Fahrenheit in summer to below zero at times in winter. The floors of the steep-sided canyons are scattered with sagebrush, cactus, and a few grasses tenacious enough to survive aridity and the short growing season. There are few year-round streams, and rainfall—scarcely 10 inches a year in the valleys and 15 inches over the higher mesa tops—is unreliable.

The Chaco Anasazi used stone axes like the one at right to cut the more than 200,000 trees needed to construct the canyon's Great Houses. Tools of this type first appeared during the Basket Maker period. They have heads of pecked and sharpened stone and may be hafted with stems and fiber from the yucca plant.

Moreover, the rain is not always a blessing to the land. Summer storms can produce flash floods that send torrents rushing down canyons, scouring away the thin, fragile topsoil. Even for modern, high-technology farmers, agriculture is at best a marginal proposition.

The climate was no gentler 800 years ago. Yet by AD 1100, the Anasazi had not only found sufficient ecological space in their difficult environment to live in reasonable com-

124

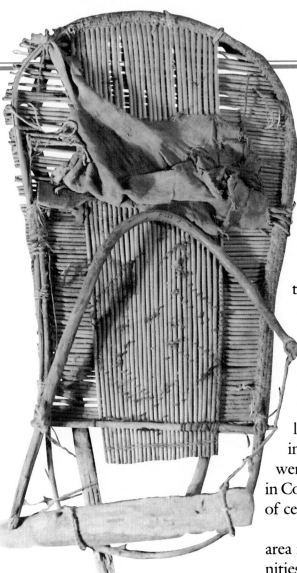

Around AD 750, in a significant change from the Basket Maker practice, Anasazi women began strapping newborns into rigid, unpadded cradleboards, causing permanent cranial deformation. No one knows for sure why this change took place.

Traditionally woven from yucca fiber or Apocynum, *sandals were the Anasazis' most important article of clothing. Worn since early Basket Maker times, they protected feet from rocks, cactus, and insects.*

fort, but they had also developed one of the most advanced cultures in North America outside Mexico. The vast and exquisite pueblos, with room for hundreds of families, and the cliff houses—whole apartment blocks squeezed into caves set high on canyon walls—were only the most obvious Anasazi achievements. Lesser stone-built villages, some with scores of dwellings, some with only two or three, were spread across their territory like seeds broadcast by a desert plant.

By mid-1992, archaeologists had identified 22,000 distinct sites in New Mexico alone and speculated that the true total might be nearer 100,000. Several consist of massive structures, appearing from a distance to be still intact; others are no more than low mounds, often marked only by telltale clumps of wolfberry, a tough shrub that thrives on disturbed ground. Known sites extend over more than 25,000 square miles of the Four Corners region. Recent evidence suggests that "Anasaziland"—if the name is used to mean an area of cultural predominance, not a political entity—may have been even larger. There were three branches: Chaco Canyon in New Mexico, Mesa Verde in Colorado, and Kayenta in northeastern Arizona, differing in styles of ceramics and architecture but sharing a common culture.

Pottery, jewelry, and other artifacts found throughout the area reveal the extent of trade links among distant Anasazi communities—and with the cultures of Mexico. High-tech archaeological tools, such as remote sensing *(page 133)* and computer-enhanced aerial photography, have revealed an estimated 400 miles of ancient roadway—all constructed by a people without draft animals or the wheel—stretching north to south from the Rockies to the Mogollon Mountains, and a somewhat lesser distance from east to west.

The Anasazi also bequeathed to the future much evidence of almost every aspect of their material culture. The dry mountain climate of the Southwest helped greatly; everything from 1,400-year-old baskets and sandals to human remains and the furs and fabrics that clothed the dead are far better preserved than similarly fragile remains from the contemporary Mound Builder cultures of the eastern United States, where moisture took a heavy toll.

At Canyon de Chelly in northeast Arizona, archaeologists uncovered a particularly evocative burial. In a grave at the base of the canyon wall lay the

TURQUOISE: THE COLOR OF MONEY

The settlement of the Anasazi in a harsh, dry land and their increasing dependence on agriculture forced them to find ways to provide for their growing population during times when food was scarce. Some archaeologists believe that one way they did so was through trade with other communities, both within their own domain and with groups as far away as central Mexico and the Gulf of California.

The discovery at New Mexico's Chaco Canyon of more than 500,000 pieces of turquoise, many of them fashioned into beads and pendants, long puzzled archaeologists. The quantity seemed to exceed any need the inhabitants might have had for personal adornment. Moreover, turquoise would have been hard for them to obtain, with the nearest mine more than 100 miles away, near modern Santa Fe. Some students of the Anasazi now believe that turquoise served them as a medium of exchange, rather like money, enabling them to obtain a variety of items they might otherwise have been unable to acquire.

Macaw feathers, copper bells,

A vibrantly colored apronlike garment made of macaw feathers and squirrel fur indicates far-ranging trade by the Anasazi. Brought to light in a Utah cave, it is thought to have been produced in the 12th century by an artisan using feathers imported from Mesoamerica, the macaw's habitat.

Copper bells like these Mexican ones were no doubt prized by the Anasazi, who lacked metallurgy. Found in New Mexico, they date to about AD 1000.

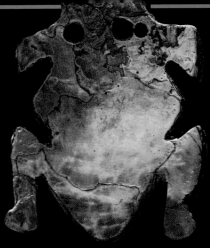

and Pacific Coast shells are just some of the exotic objects found in Anasazi territory that point to trade with far-off groups. The most likely transactions, however, involved durable goods and food. This conclusion is borne out by the presence at various sites of potsherds from ceramics produced well beyond the area and, at Chaco, by a far greater number of what appear to be food storerooms than dwellings.

Scholars have suggested over the years that some aspects of Anasazi culture were directly stimulated by the more advanced civilizations of Mexico. But, given the unique achievements of the Anasazi and the length of time over which they developed, experts today consider their culture to have been a homegrown one, not the product of exportation or colonization.

A Mesa Verde frog pendant, fashioned from iridescent abalone shell in the 12th century, substantiates Anasazi trading ties with the Pacific Coast, where the shellfish are found.

A cylindrical basketry tube inlaid with pieces of turquoise is just one of the unusual luxury items excavated in 1896 at Chaco Canyon's Pueblo Bonito by the Hyde Exploring Expedition. The artifacts found filled an entire freight car.

The significance to the Anasazi of this unusual and ingenious container, which was found during excavations in Chaco Canyon, is unknown. The flanged lid covered a hand-cut stone bowl filled with 146 turquoise beads.

body of an old man curled in the fetal position, his graying hair pulled back in a ponytail. He wore a cloak made of golden-eagle down and two cotton blankets, one of which, despite its age, looked brand-new. A single ear of corn rested on his chest. The quantity of belongings surrounding the body led excavators to believe that the man had been highly esteemed in his community. Along with a large, powerful bow and a single wood-tipped arrow, five pottery jars and four woven baskets lined the grave. They contained piñon nuts, beans, salt, and corn in all its daily usages—husked, shelled, and ground into meal. The most conclusive indication of the man's livelihood was cotton yarn wound in thick skeins—more than two miles of it—and a wooden spindle used to spin the cotton into thread. Archaeologists have dubbed this illuminating discovery the Burial of the Weaver.

The quantity of evidence from Canyon de Chelly and elsewhere is as impressive as its quality; between 1976 and 1978, for example, one relatively modest excavation covering less than 10 percent of a two-acre site at Chaco Canyon turned up more than 200,000 different artifacts, ranging from tiny potsherds to burned roof timbers that would help date the site.

The temporal extent of the Anasazi tradition matches its geographical dimensions. Archaeologists have traced a cultural evolution that dates back to the first century AD, when the forebears of the Anasazi emerged as a distinct, settled group from the nomadic desert foragers who had sparsely inhabited the Southwest for millennia. These early Anasazi lived simply, in meager shelters built in the open that after almost 2,000 years are hard to distinguish from random scatterings of stones. But they also took advantage of some of the region's caves, possibly using them as living quarters but certainly as storehouses and burial grounds. In one such cave in a Utah canyon Richard Wetherill found the Basket Maker skeletons that so excited him back in December 1893.

The progression from the earliest settlements through increasingly advanced Basket Maker intermediaries to the builders of the great pueblos took centuries—and the task of identifying and separating the various milestones in the development of Anasazi culture was likewise protracted. In the century since Wetherill brought the Anasazi to the attention of the general public and the scientific community, generations of American archaeologists—

from educated amateurs like Bandelier to today's university-trained specialists—have cut their professional teeth in Anasazi country.

Meanwhile, anthropologists were learning more about the region's living Native American cultures, especially the Zuni and the Hopi. Their way of life, their art and architecture, all mirrored what was known of the Anasazi through archaeological research. Pueblo tribes had endured major upheavals over the preceding centuries—first Spanish, then American, conquest, with accompanying slaughter, disease, and the tradition-eroding work of proselytizing missionaries—but through it all they maintained sufficient cultural identity to permit scientists to identify them unreservedly as direct Anasazi descendants. Southwestern culture could thus trace an unbroken line of development over almost two millennia.

By the 1920s, archaeologists had more than enough raw data on the Anasazi to digest. They needed some kind of framework, a cultural sequence that would help them make sense of their discoveries. In 1927, southwestern archaeologists gathered at Pecos, New Mexico, for the first of what eventually became annual conferences. High on their agenda was an agreed terminology that would place a firm chronology on the peoples they studied.

Basket Maker I became the designation for the people of the hypothetical pre-agricultural period, precursors to the Basket Maker II people, who depended somewhat on farming. The Pecos classification continued, from Basket Maker III, pit-house builders and the first potters, to Pueblo I, the first aboveground dwellers, all the way through Pueblo III, when the Anasazi settlements in the Four Corners region were abandoned. Pueblo IV continued the sequence with the florescence of Anasazi culture in the Rio Grande Basin. Pueblo V became the classification that covered historic tribes from AD 1600 to the present.

Mummy Cave, named for the human remains found there during a 19th-century expedition, sits a hundred feet above an ancient shard-littered path. This Arizona site in Canyon de Chelly contains a large Anasazi cliff dwelling, including the structure pictured, which has 15 rooms and a three-story tower.

In 1936, Alfred V. Kidder suggested the name "Anasazi" to describe the entire Basket Maker-Pueblo cultural development, thereby differentiating it from the Hohokam and the Mogollon and other southwestern traditions. It was not, modern archaeologists agree, an ideal choice. The blanket term *Anasazi* certainly reinforces the idea of a common culture, but it also implies an exaggerated degree of affinity between all Anasazi groups, lumping them together as a single homogeneous—and extinct—tribe. Without written records, it is impossible to know whether the peoples spread throughout Anasaziland considered themselves one tribe or many, or even spoke the same language; certainly it is impossible to know what they called themselves. And since their descendants still live in the same area, they can hardly be called extinct. However, the name stuck and no one has been able to come up with a convenient alternative.

Basket Maker communities came to rely upon planted crops for survival; their regional population levels were probably too high to be sustained by hunting and gathering alone in such arid territory, where wild resources would have been few and far between. This dependence on agriculture brought about fundamental changes in the Anasazi lifestyle, including the need to remain in one place for much longer periods of time.

Archaeologists at Mesa Verde discovered this cluster of early-seventh-century Basket Maker pit houses buried under the ruins of cliff dwellings erected 600 years later. The pit house at upper right has been partially reconstructed to illustrate what the structures looked like. Few of the baskets for which these early Anasazi were named remain; the container at right was made between AD 500 and 700.

The rudimentary shelters of the Basket Maker II camp were superseded by the pit house. The Anasazi who settled in Chaco Canyon around AD 500 lived in simple dwellings on the elevated mesas above where the Great Houses would rise four centuries later. By excavating these early sites, archaeologists have pieced together the building process. First, the Anasazi would gouge a shallow depression in the earth, lining the perimeter with flat stones placed upright or with mud plaster. Log sections formed the walls of the house, and wooden poles running from wall to wall, chinked with adobe, formed the roof. Most pit houses contained a basin-shaped firepit—a hollow in the floor used for cooking and heating.

Canyon de Chelly was, thanks to a reliable stream and to fertile soil in the canyon bottom, a very early focal point of the Basket Maker culture. The high, dry caves that punctuate the sheer sandstone walls of the canyon provided excellent winter shelter. The caves—with ideal climatic conditions for the archaeologist—have handed down to modern researchers more examples of the Basket Makers' weaving prowess than any other Anasazi locale. A tree-ring date obtained from one alcove definitively fixes Anasazi occupation to AD 306, but earlier piles of sweepings and ashes at the site suggest that it may have been inhabited during the preceding three centuries.

Despite their shift to agriculture, the Basket Makers had not completely abandoned the gathering techniques of their nomadic ancestors. In a land whose resources were always slender and uncertain, they could not afford to overlook any potential food source. Excavations have turned up piñon nuts and Indian rice grass in Basket Maker storage pits. The men continued to hunt as well. With the additional leverage given by a wooden spear-thrower—known to archaeologists by its Aztec name, *atlatl*—hunters could hurl a six-foot spear with enough force to bring down a deer, an antelope, or a bighorn sheep at 100 yards' range. Rabbits, however, probably provided more meat than any other species.

Gaming pieces made of bone sometimes turn up at Basket Maker sites. This set, complete with its leather carrying bag, was found in a Utah cave. Some of the pieces are incised; others have holes drilled in them. Thrown like dice, they offered 44 possible combinations.

A network of prehistoric roads, buried and invisible from the ground, stands sharply etched in the landscape of Chaco Canyon in an aerial image (right) captured by a thermal infrared multispectral scanner. Combined with other factors, the compressed dirt of the roadbeds retains more heat than the adjacent soil and therefore registers a higher temperature—represented by the color blue—on the scanner. A recently developed computer database, known as Geographic Information Systems (GIS), can combine such remotely obtained data with ancillary data such as topographic maps to generate a three-dimensional site model (below). Archaeologists can manipulate and analyze the display on their terminal screens.

MODERN ROAD

PREHISTORIC ROADS

PREHISTORIC ROADS

PUEBLO ALTO

PUEBLO ALTO

LOFTY EVIDENCE OF LONG-BURIED CULTURES

The sands of time have concealed many traces of North America's pre-Columbian cultures. But space-age technology has helped scientists discover buried earthworks, roadways, walls, and buildings—features undetectable by the human eye.

Since the beginning of the 20th century, archaeologists have used airborne cameras fastened to balloons or kites to gain a loftier perspective on their digs. In 1929 Charles Lindbergh took the archaeologist Alfred V. Kidder on numerous flights, including surveys of New Mexico's Chaco Canyon. And a 1934 aerial photograph of Poverty Point, Louisiana, remained for almost five decades the best overall guide to that site's intricate arrangement of earthworks, the earliest mounds in the Southeast.

These initial efforts, while providing a worthwhile bird's-eye view, nevertheless had their limitations. Conventional photographs record only the narrow band of visible light in the electromagnetic spectrum. But new sensing devices detect a much broader range of otherwise imperceptible wavelengths. Carried aloft in airplanes and satellites, these remote sensors offer ways to "see" hidden details in the earth below.

Buried prehistoric structures sometimes affect the temperature of the soil above them. Stone walls or heavily compacted roadways, for example, soak up more of the sun's heat, resulting in measurably higher surface temperatures. The looser soil of earthen mounds or filled-in canals will, conversely, retain more moisture, thereby creating cooler temperatures.

Remote infrared sensors trained on archaeological sites can recognize such temperature patterns. As seen in the three images shown here, these patterns vividly emerge when unnatural, brightly contrasting colors are assigned to different levels of infrared emission—a process called false-color imaging. With such sophisticated tools to guide them, today's archaeologists can eliminate much of the exploratory, frequently unproductive digging that previously characterized their fieldwork.

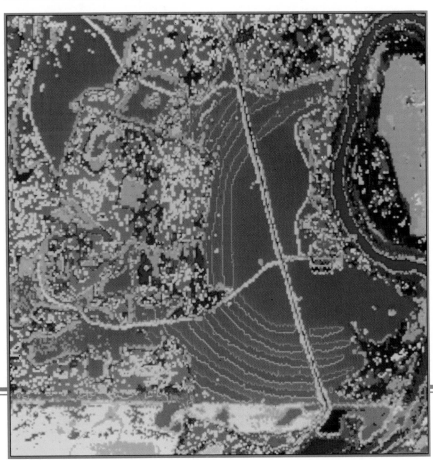

Taken from a NASA *jet in 1984, this infrared image shows the six concentric earthwork ridges* (red) *surrounding a 1,200-meter enclosure* (green) *at Poverty Point, a 3,500-year-old site on a bluff above Bayou Macon* (blue, at right of image) *in northeastern Louisiana. The ridges, though now largely eroded, contain remains of human activity that produce subtle variations in temperature detectable by remote sensors.*

Slipnoose snares and nets, made of human hair, have been found in rock shelters. Archaeologists discovered one ambitious game trap while excavating White Dog Cave near Kayenta, in northeastern Arizona. Resembling a tennis net, it is 240 feet long, three feet wide, and made from almost four miles of human hair and *Apocynum,* commonly known as Indian hemp. How many man-hours (or, more likely, woman-hours) it took to weave can only be imagined, but its deployment, probably across a canyon mouth to entangle driven prey, must have required a major cooperative effort, possibly involving more than one hamlet.

For most of the Basket Maker period, communities were small: perhaps between six and 10 pit houses with their accompanying storage units, occasionally sheltered beneath the cliff overhang. Often a settlement would be abandoned after a generation or two and another created nearby, as weathered adobe could not be repaired or rebuilt. Some old settlement sites might well have been reoccupied within a century or so. Such moves were almost certainly prompted by modest variations in microclimate and soil drainage patterns. An extra half-inch of rainfall or a patch of earth that retained water one week longer could make the difference between life and death.

Corn, introduced from Mexico, provided the basis of the Anasazi diet. Even during the early Basket Maker period, selective propagation by the Anasazi themselves and the arrival of improved seedstock from the south produced ears almost the size of modern corn. Most years the people harvested and stored sufficient grain to pursue cultural activities.

Thanks to well-preserved burials like that of the weaver at Canyon de Chelly, researchers have a good knowledge of what these early Anasazi looked like. Small by modern standards—the men averaged just over five feet—they were racially akin, perhaps almost identical, to modern southwestern Indians, with brown skin and either straight or wavy black hair. The men usually kept their hair long and tied back; the women sacrificed theirs as raw material for cord making and netting.

Again from the evidence of the graves, Basket Maker clothing was minimal, sometimes amounting to no more than a pair of sandals woven from yucca fiber for the men, with women also wearing a string or fiber

This burial cist in a Utah cave may have contained one or more bodies along with clothing, baskets, and other personal belongings. While the Anasazi buried their dead in a number of different places— caves, cists, or middens—the manner of arranging the body was usually the same: arms and legs flexed against the chest with head oriented toward the east.

apron. In winter, people protected themselves from the biting cold with hide cloaks and shirts, and with blankets made from twined rabbit fur. What they lacked in clothing they made up for in ornamentation. Beads of jet and argillite stone, abalone shell, bone, and polished seeds were commonplace, usually strung into necklaces. Feathers figured as hair adornments, pendants, and sometimes as trim for fur robes. As the culture of the Basket Makers endured—more than 500 years over most of their territory— clothing became more elaborate, with braided sashes and finely woven aprons. In the Basket Maker III period, sandals were scallop-toed and decorated with colored figures and ornate knots.

Side-by-side metates, *rock troughs used for grinding corn, show that food preparation was often a communal activity. With smaller stones called* manos, *women ground the staple into meal or flour that then could be made into stews, gruel, or flatbreads. Granaries* (above right) *shielded stored food from moisture and pests.*

Around AD 600, perhaps because of their advancing technology (the Anasazi had adopted the bow for hunting), or perhaps because of a slightly more favorable climate, the population seems to have increased. At any rate, the Basket Maker villages began, literally, to rise out of the ground. From the late eighth and ninth centuries, their small surface storage structures had larger, domestic quarters of stone and adobe built onto them, a process of architectural accretion that culminated in multiroomed houses, usually arranged in a solid arc on two or three sides of an open work area or plaza. The flat roofs, accessible by wooden ladders, functioned as additional work areas for cooking, drying food, and painting pottery.

It was a major step forward. No eighth-century Anasazi, of course, was aware of crossing a threshold from "Basket Maker III" to "Pueblo I," but the transformation was nonetheless abrupt. The transition was clear to the 20th-century archaeologists who would give the cultures their names, yet the very magnitude of the change led early investigators into a serious mistake.

Working backward through time, they had discovered traces

135

Tucked into a spectacular 500-foot-high natural amphitheater, the 13th-century cliff dwelling of Betatakin is as enigmatic as it is breathtaking. The 135-room site in Arizona was erected, enlarged, and then abandoned—all within the timespan of two generations.

of the Basket Makers only after they had excavated the more complex ruins of their successors. For many years these researchers, like Wetherill, were convinced that the pueblo dwellers were a completely different people. They displayed a new, far more complex architecture, had abundant pottery, and understood the use of the bow and arrow. All this seemed to point to a vigorous incoming culture that had overwhelmed and replaced the more primitive Basket Makers.

The clincher was a startling anatomical difference between the early Pueblo people and the Basket Makers they had apparently supplanted. Instead of the long, narrow heads characteristic of their predecessors, the early Pueblo people had very different, broad heads. In fact, as subsequent analysis of skeletal remains would show, the change was the result not of genetics but of fashion. The Basket Makers used soft, padded cradleboards for their infants; the Pueblo people preferred hard boards that physically flattened their children's pliable, growing skulls. It is impossible to know for sure why the deformation—or beauty treatment—was adopted: contact with flat-headed outsiders whom the Anasazi respected, perhaps, or imitation of Anasazi leaders whose heads were naturally flattened. At any rate, the new skull style clearly had immense appeal, for within a short time it had spread throughout the entire Anasazi area, enduring as long as the Anasazi themselves.

Another fundamental transition during the early Pueblo phase involved the role of the pit house. Though seldom used as living areas, pit houses did not disappear from Anasazi settlements;

136

quite the contrary, they became ubiquitous throughout the Anasazi homeland. Usually smaller and dug deeper than the former Basket Maker dwellings, these semisubterranean chambers were situated in the plaza of the pueblo and now assumed a ceremonial function. In fact, they bear a very close resemblance to structures used by the Hopi, the Zuni, and other contemporary Pueblo tribes for religious rituals and secular events. The Hopi name for this underground room is *kiva*, and archaeologists rapidly adopted the term to describe the ancestral Anasazi equivalent.

Most scholars are prepared to assume that Anasazi kivas served the same purpose as Hopi and Zuni kivas do today. Restricted

Pots sitting on a wall at Arizona's Kiet Siel look as though their owners left them there just moments before. Scattered potsherds and corncobs also serve to make this large, well-preserved ruin seem recently occupied. But like Betatakin, its Kayenta-area neighbor, Kiet Siel has been deserted for 700 years.

to the initiated menfolk (women are admitted for special ceremonies), they are at once religious centers and clubhouses for the numerous "societies" in the villages, each devoted to a particular aspect of daily or religious life—or both, since the two are inseparable. From the time of its appearance right up to today, the kiva has been an unmistakable cultural indicator, marking a settlement as clearly as a signpost. By the 12th century—the Pueblo III period— each village had one or more kivas, with a smoke hole in the roof and a ladder serving as the only entry into a chamber lined with masonry and furnished with a wall bench, wall niches, and often a curious sand-filled hole in the floor, which most scholars suspect probably corresponds to the *sipapu* of modern Pueblo belief. The archaeologist Bill Sweetland of Bandelier National Monument refers to the kiva as the "middle ground between the living and the spirits of their ancestors," with the sipapu serving as the "entrance" for the latter. Unlike their contemporaries, the Mississippians, the Anasazi seem to have had no fear of the underworld; it was their indirect equivalent of heaven, a dwelling place for the souls of the deceased.

All of the Great Houses in Chaco Canyon, that extraordinary hub of Anasazi culture, include numerous kivas—Pueblo Bonito alone contains at least 32. The Great Houses of Chaco have fascinated scholars and laymen alike since they were described by Lieutenant Simpson in 1849. Twentieth-century advances in scientific techniques have revealed much new information—and corrected earlier misconceptions—about them. Construction and occupancy dates have been precisely established, mainly by means of the tree-ring chronology developed by Douglass in the 1920s, but also with the help of newer techniques that measure the magnetic alignment of particles of burned clay. By matching the alignment to the known shift in the earth's own magnetic poles over time, archaeologists can

Cool and serene, the interior of the only completely restored Great Kiva conveys a solemnity befitting its sacred purpose. In the 12th century, the inhabitants of this New Mexico site—called Aztec Ruins—built the kiva and a 500-room residential complex in the Chacoan Style.

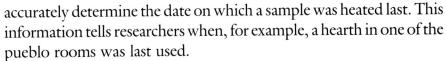

accurately determine the date on which a sample was heated last. This information tells researchers when, for example, a hearth in one of the pueblo rooms was last used.

At first, archaeologists considered the Great Houses to be prehistoric apartment buildings, with a total canyon population estimated as high as 10,000. Such an interpretation made Chaco a genuine urban center, and one that would have put an appalling strain on its fragile environment—although the Anasazi had learned how to make the most of the erratic rains. Even so, it was hard to see how the Chaco district could have supported so many people. A team of archaeologists began excavations in 1976 at Pueblo Alto on the northern rim of Chaco Canyon and turned up some astounding data. Judged mainly by the presence of a functioning hearth—a winter necessity at Chaco—scarcely one in 20 of the pueblo's rooms displayed evidence of domestic use, and most of those dated from the earliest construction phase. Permanent inhabitants of all the Great Houses put together could be counted in hundreds, not thousands.

There were other anomalies. One single excavation trench in a trash mound at Pueblo Alto yielded no fewer than 70,000 artifacts, mostly broken pottery; archaeologists estimated that over a period of 60 years, bits and pieces of 150,000 clay vessels had been added to the midden—a colossal wastage for only 100 or so full-time residents. Moreover, the excavated potsherds were found in clearly separated layers, suggesting that at intervals Pueblo Alto had been the scene of some sort of mass ceremonial trashing. One interpretation now views the Great Houses of Chaco as sites for periodic gatherings of Anasazi from the whole San Juan Basin: ceremonial assemblies at least somewhat analogous to religious pilgrimages or trade fairs.

Chaco may even have had an astronomical function. Modern Hopi and Zuni Indians employ solar observations to plant crops and determine their ritual calendar, and archaeologists are certain that their Anasazi forebears had similar information. Some researchers point to the unusual number of corner doors and windows in Pueblo Bonito, two of which have been shown to mark the sun's position on the winter solstice. Evidence from other sites in and around the canyon is more ambiguous. Nevertheless, according to the archaeological team of Robert and Florence Lister, "The consensus is that Chacoans used astronomical phenomena as a basis for regulating the annual round of religious rites and for predicting seasonal changes that would affect the cleaning and repair of irrigation works, the preparation of the fields, and the planting of crops."

Whatever the astronomical skills of its people, there is no doubt that Chaco in its prime was a great trading center. Much of the fragmented pottery came from distant sources, especially the Chuska area, almost 40 miles westward. But Chaco's main specialty was turquoise, held in high regard by all Anasazi groups: Hundreds of turquoise artifacts, and tiny fragments of the blue stone by the thousands, have been found in the canyon. Some archaeologists argue that turquoise had great ritual importance, and that regular visits to Chaco to obtain it were a vital part of Anasazi religious life.

Toward the end of the Basket Maker period—well before the Chaco heyday—the Ana-

This well-preserved cliff dwelling in a Utah canyon is one of many that have not been extensively excavated or studied. Scattered throughout the Southwest are thousands of such ruins containing artifacts like the corrugated pot at right. Disturbing these remains is illegal, since the overall effect of each visitor's removing even one potsherd would be to skew the archaeological profile of the site.

sazi had made an important discovery. Earlier Anasazi cooks, with no fire-resistant cauldrons to place directly on the flames, had plunged hot rocks into baskets filled with water or gruel. Sometimes the baskets were made leakproof with daubs of pitch; more often, the weave itself and the expansion of damp fibers created a watertight seal. Then, sometime before AD 500, the Anasazi learned how to make pottery in a smothered fire, whose oxygen-free environment produced a practical ware with a characteristic gray-white finish. Foods that were troublesome or impossible to prepare by the hot-stone method could now be cooked and stored with relative ease. Beans, for example, need to be soaked and boiled; interestingly, their first appearance among the plants cultivated by the Anasazi coincides with the arrival of pottery.

As the Pueblo period progressed, pottery became more sophisticated, with black-on-white coloring replacing both plain gray or black on gray, even in everyday ware. Cooking pots were often

made up of successive rings of clay—no pre-Columbian culture ever developed the potter's wheel—producing a corrugated effect that was at once visually attractive, prevented slippage when carried, and also improved heat transfer from a cooking fire to the pots' contents.

Modern scientific techniques—including neutron activation analysis, which can link a piece of pottery to a clay source by means of a unique "fingerprint" of radioactive trace elements—have shown that pottery was often produced a long way from where it was unearthed. In Chaco Canyon especially, most of the ware originated in other parts of the Anasazi domain. Imported or home produced, it was exquisitely decorated. Basic gray pots were finished in fine, white (and very occasionally, red) clay, then black paint was applied. Sometimes Anasazi artists portrayed human figures; more often, they preferred complex geometric patterns. Similar designs have been found painted on rocks and walls, especially kiva walls, and many more may have faded or eroded over the centuries.

There is some evidence of trade links with the contemporary civilization far to the south in present-day Mexico. Certain Chaco pottery designs appear to reflect Mexican motifs, and other, more tangible items also suggest contacts: copper bells, for example, and the skeletons of macaws. Brightly colored macaw feathers had an important role in both Maya and Toltec ritual; the Anasazi may have used them for similar purposes.

The Mexican connection may only have been sporadic, but recent research is steadily extending the size of the Chaco network. Aerial surveys have revealed traces of Chaco-style Great Houses, mostly eroded to rubble, over a much wider area than had previously been imagined. Archaeologists are beginning to suspect that the zone of Chaco Anasazi influence might have extended over much of the 25,000-square-mile San Juan Basin, and possibly beyond.

The Chaco high point occurred between AD 1075 and 1115, when the final phase of Great House construction was completed. Despite the effort that had gone into its creation, the Chaco Phenomenon—as archaeologists refer to it—was sadly short-lived. According to the tree-ring record, dry year followed dry year in dismal succession. W. James Judge, former director of the U.S. National Park Service's long-term Chaco Project, implies that, because of the worsening conditions, Chaco Canyon may have lost its role as a

CHACO CANYON ANASAZI: EARLY WATCHERS OF THE SKY

July 4, 1054, marked the advent of a supernova, a stellar explosion of such magnitude that it remained visible in the daytime sky the world over for three weeks and at night for almost two years. This unusual event occurred during one of the most intense building periods of the Chaco Canyon Anasazi and undoubtedly was observed by them.

Astronomers and archaeologists studying the cultures of the area have long supposed that the prehistoric residents were dedicated sky watchers. The discovery in the early 1970s by an archaeological survey team of a rock painting that may portray the supernova suggests the impact such a celestial event could well have had on the inhabitants of Anasaziland.

The find is a reddish brown pictograph on a sandstone overhang below the ruined Chaco Canyon pueblo of Penasco Blanco. The glyph consists of a hand, which may indicate the sacredness of the spot, a star, and a crescent. Below these symbols is a possible depiction of the sun, three concentric circles around a dot. According to the archaeoastronomer Ray A. Williamson, the glyph very closely "reproduces the astronomical circumstances of July 4, 1054"—a star, the supernova itself, appearing south of a crescent moon, with the sun below the horizon.

Because the pictograph cannot be dated conclusively, Williamson's theory may never be universally accepted. Scholars do agree, however, that in many ways astronomy pervaded Anasazi life, influencing the timing of their rituals, hunting, and farming, and even the orientation of their homes.

Framing the morning sun, a window at New Mexico's Casa Rinconada (above) *may have served to confirm the summer solstice. A similar device, known as the sun dagger, formed by a slit in the rock through which a sunbeam passed onto a spiral petroglyph, performed such a function at New Mexico's Fajada Butte* (left). *By tracking the sun's yearly journey across the horizon, the Anasazi would have been able to forecast the timing of the solstices.*

Possibly a record of the supernova known as the Crab Nebula, this petroglyph shows the starlike body south of the crescent moon whose tips point to the west, the position both objects would have had on the morning of July 4, 1054. The moon's phase for the day was confirmed by computer analysis.

focus for trade pilgrimages and ritual and become more residential.

Chaco had survived droughts before: During the final building surge, temporary failures in summer rainfall had put the agricultural system under strain. Then, there had been enough stored food to see the resident community through a few hungry years. But this time, the drought went on far longer: For half a century, precipitation remained substantially below average. The environmental deterioration became too severe for the weakened Chacoan infrastructure to handle, and people began to leave.

The two other great Anasazi centers, in the San Juan Basin and near Kayenta, lagged behind Chaco in time but had notable developmental features of their own. For example, pottery styles (though still in the classic Anasazi black-on-white mode) and architecture were distinctly different.

In contrast to the treeless, relatively shallow valley of Chaco, the Anasazi of the northern San Juan lived among forests of juniper and piñon, on top of broad mesas, or in high, open valleys. Their most spectacular legacy remains the huge cliff dwellings at Mesa Verde, 140 miles north of Chaco Canyon, but the region contains at least eight large Pueblo III villages, each with a population exceeding 1,000. At the height of the Pueblo III phase, there may have been 30,000 to 40,000 people living in the area—twice as many as in modern southwestern Colorado. The greatest concentration was at Yellow Jacket, today a sprawling ruin. The Yellow Jacket site includes 1,826 rooms arranged around four plazas, with 166 kivas and a Great Kiva of a size comparable to Chaco's largest.

The climate made agriculture less precarious than at Chaco, and dryland farming, which relied only on natural rainfall, was possible on the mesa tops. Even so, the high population required the usual careful Anasazi water management. Yellow Jacket had a reservoir and a spillway dam; at Mesa Verde, more than 1,000 stone-check dams have been located. Built to

An overhanging sandstone brow protects Mesa Verde's Cliff Palace from the onslaught of winter. Snowfalls totaling 80 to 100 inches a year account for much of the annual precipitation at Mesa Verde. Since the area lacks year-round running streams, snowmelt helped to prepare the ground for spring planting.

slow runoff from both summer storms and melting winter snow, the dams also served another purpose: They trapped soil brought down with the rushing water and gave their custodians additional small but fertile gardens.

The San Juan area was inhabited at least as long as other Anasazi territories, and its people passed through the same developmental phases. The cliff dwellings that so excited early visitors constituted the last stage of Anasazi culture in the region. Construction of the Mesa Verde phase began about 1070; between then and the early 1200s, many San Juan settlements moved from open mesa locations to the extraordinary new lodgings they had built for themselves, wedged like swallows' nests in canyonside recesses.

One seemingly obvious motive for such a shift would be defense, but there are only sporadic signs of warfare or warlike preparations throughout the entire Anasazi period. The need to nourish an increased population might offer a better explanation. By transferring living space from potentially fertile mesa tops and canyon floors, Anasazi farmers could increase the area of cultivable ground. Gains would have been marginal, perhaps, but even in the relatively fertile San Juan Basin, the Anasazi always lived close to the margin.

The third major grouping was to the west, around Kayenta, about 120 miles northeast of Flagstaff, Arizona. The Kayenta Anasazi entered their pueblo-building period somewhat later than the others. According to Gary Matlock, an archaeologist with the U.S. Forest Service, "If the Northern San Juan Anasazi area served as the breadbasket and Chaco as the great trade center, the Kayenta area can perhaps be characterized as the Anasazi Bohemia." They were excellent potters and artisans, but their settlements appear somewhat second-rate compared with their cousins'. While some Anasazi groups elsewhere were building large-scale communities, the Kayenta group put its energies into westward expansion, settling substantial new territory for a century or so from about AD 1000.

Expansion ended around 1150, most likely because of decreasing rainfall and other environmental problems. Many westward settlements were abandoned; pueblos in the Kayenta heartland increased in size to accommodate the dispossessed, and much effort had to be devoted to soil and water engineering. Toward the end of the 13th century, the margins finally became too tight. Between 1286 and 1300, according to tree-ring dating, the Kayenta Anasazi packed up and left. They took with them almost everything that could be carried; some households even sealed up their doors, perhaps in the hope of an eventual return. As it turned out, they never did, but neither did the residents move any great distance. "The important concept is that the Kayenta area as a whole has never really been abandoned," says Matlock. "The Kayenta display the closest relationship of any Anasazi group to modern Pueblo Indians. The Hopi continue to exhibit a nearly full range of Anasazi cultural traits."

Elsewhere in the Four Corners region, the landscape could no longer sustain its human burden, at least not in the concentrations reached by the end of the 13th century. The Anasazi themselves might have contributed to what modern ecologists would call "environmental degradation" through the agricultural intensification caused by higher regional populations.

Additional problems were caused by another Anasazi activity—tree felling. Rain washed the earth from the naturally forested

The Anasazi of the arid Hovenweep region built their masonry villages near permanent springs using sandstone outcrops for foundations. The function of Hovenweep's unusual towers is uncertain—theories include bastions, ceremonial centers, and observatories.

mesa tops, where the workings of the forest ecology steadily renewed it. But the Anasazi were under constant pressure to clear the mesa tops. They needed the space for growing crops, and they needed the wood as building material as well as fuel for cooking, pottery firing, and winter heating.

Drought, falling yields, shortages of wood for construction and for fires—in combination, they spelled the end of the Anasazi experiment. Everywhere, the collapse was a gentle one; the Anasazi may have overexploited their environment, but their numbers were relatively low and so was their technology. They had wrought their destruction slowly, and the price they paid for it did not include catastrophe. Doubtless some Anasazi starved. Children died who would in better times have grown to adulthood. And many who survived carried the effects of malnutrition into adulthood. But there was no overnight disaster, no population crash. Chaco, always a marginal proposition in the best of times, was abandoned first; Mesa Verde migrants appear to have settled briefly in the empty canyon buildings before the continuing drought made life there impossible. Finally defeated by their desert environment, family by family, kin group by kin group, they moved off in search of a better life.

The Kayenta people headed south; they are still there. The fate of the San Juan and the Chaco Anasazi is a little more obscure, but it is probable that they moved on to the Bandelier area and the pueblos that dot the Rio Grande Valley. As Anasazi, the Old Ones, the Enemy Ancestors, they had vanished from the earth. As Hopi, Zuni, and the other Pueblo tribes, they had a long future.

The Anasazi culture at Bandelier persevered much longer, thanks, in part, to a wetter climate and to an eons-old geologic cataclysm. More than a million years ago, a volcano in the Jemez Mountains west of Bandelier had blown up, creating a caldera 28 miles across and depositing a layer of ash 600 to 1,000 feet deep over the 450-square-mile landscape. Compressed over a vast span of time, the ash became volcanic tuff, the soft stone into which the Anasazi gouged the cave dwellings that so amazed Adolph Bandelier. On the flat mesa tops and in the canyon bottoms, untold millennia of rain and erosion had transformed the tuff into moisture-retaining soil. In some places, small pebbles of light-colored pumice form an insulating top layer that reflects the sun's heat. Even on hot, cloudless days the soil beneath this layer remains cool and moist to the touch. Pointing to a dry saddle between two mesas that contain extensive Anasazi caves, the archaeologist Bill Sweetland maintains that "we could grow corn here today."

According to Sweetland, the Anasazi would usually plant corn, beans, and squash in the same hole. The squash would come up first, spreading out to provide ground cover. The corn would emerge next, its stalk shooting up through the squash and providing a convenient pole for the later-germinating bean plant to climb. After harvesting, the dried cornstalk was recycled as fuel. The medley of vegetables provided a healthy diet; an enzyme in the beans released the protein in the corn and made it digestible to humans, while squash added minerals and vitamins.

A pottery fragment found at Pueblo Bonito in Chaco Canyon portrays a rare glimpse of the human form in Anasazi art. This six-inch-high piece of an effigy vessel dates from around AD 1100.

The Anasazi continued to harvest Bandelier's bounty until the same problems with soil exhaustion that had plagued other centers of their culture began to produce ever-dwindling harvests from the land. At some point not too long before the first Spanish expedition arrived in the area, the Anasazi finally deserted their caves and moved down into the Rio Grande Valley.

Today, Bandelier National Monument is ringed with Indian pueblos, including Cochiti and Santo Domingo. In Frijoles Canyon and on the nearby mesas, only memories of the Anasazi and their daily lives remain. But even a seemingly inconsequential memento of their everyday existence can inject a note of individuality into this splendid yet largely anonymous culture.

On a relatively flat, remote patch of ground beneath a row of cave dwellings, an Anasazi parent apparently carved a miniature pueblo into a waist-high boulder of volcanic tuff. Though exposure to the elements over the past six centuries has softened the lines, tiny stairways and apartment-style buildings are still discernible in the brittle

A Mesa Verde Style painted pitcher found at Chaco Canyon illustrates the prevalence of trade in Anasazi society. Archaeologists can sometimes trace the origins of pottery using chemical and physical analyses of materials. More often, they compare variations in design.

An Anasazi craftsman of the Kayenta area in Arizona carved and painted this wooden bird and its accompanying sunflowers. The objects were sealed in a clay jar and buried in a cliff dwelling, where, in the dryness, they remained perfectly preserved for more than 700 years.

rock. How this "dollhouse" must have delighted the children of the settlement. In the stillness of twilight, it is possible to imagine their laughter echoing from the cliffs as their mothers call them home for the evening meal, the glow of the cooking fires lighting their path back up the steep slope to the warm shelter of the caves.

After the Anasazi departed, the caves stood empty and forgotten by all but the Indians until an inquisitive Swiss immigrant brought them into the public eye. Before he left New Mexico, Adolph Bandelier wrote a work of historical fiction, entitled *The Delight Makers,* about Pueblo Indians prior to European contact. Published in 1890, it has been called the first anthropological novel. He explains in the preface that the first chapters were composed during his stay at the Cochiti pueblo. From the opening pages it is obvious that his foray into Frijoles Canyon and the ruins he discovered there inspired the book. Bandelier wanted to share his excitement about the Anasazi but felt that a dry scientific tome, of which he produced many, would "exercise a limited influence upon the general public." His noble aim was, as he put it, "to make the 'Truth about the Pueblo Indians' more accessible." A century later—even with many answers now available to questions that long bothered researchers—the truth, and the Anasazi, remain as tantalizingly elusive as ever.

THE WONDERS OF CHACO

In the bleak sagebrush country of north-western New Mexico lies Chaco Canyon, a broad, shallow depression indistinguishable at first glance from the surrounding plain. Yet, a thousand years ago, this drab chasm's walls embraced a remarkable cultural blossoming unsurpassed north of Mexico. But why the Anasazi chose this arid, treeless site as a locus of their society remains a mystery.

Early explorers gaped at the most visible legacy of the Anasazi presence: the colossal pueblos, some containing hundreds of rooms, that line a 10-mile stretch of the canyon. Later excavations in these so-called Great Houses uncovered a wealth of artifacts, such as the turquoise shown above, but relatively few burials. A recent archaeological study determined that only a small percentage of the Great Houses' rooms were ever occupied. Their population, once thought to be as high as 10,000, now appears to have numbered in the hundreds. Scholars, however, have not determined wheth-

er this small faction constituted an elite caste or a caretaker force, or both.

Chaco Canyon might possibly have functioned as an intermittent gathering place for Anasazi from settlements throughout the San Juan Basin. Perhaps on special occasions, people held ceremonies and rituals, exchanged goods, and renewed old friendships in the plazas of the Great Houses, while ancient legends were retold and passed on to a new generation in the kivas. Most important, the Anasazi would have found this august setting conducive to renewing their sense of unity or kinship.

Many societies create monuments to themselves, their aspirations, and their triumphs. Notwithstanding their meager resources and simple technology, the Anasazi erected a cultural hallmark in Chaco Canyon that, in its own way, rivals the grandeur of such sites as Machu Picchu, Angkor Wat, Versailles, or the Mall in Washington, D.C.

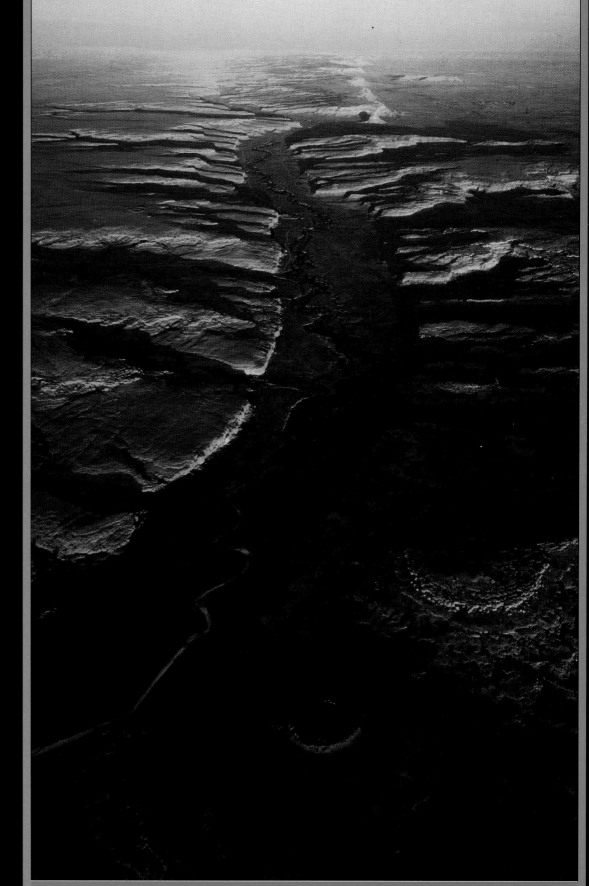

year, carved the canyon that bears its name from the region's underlying soft sandstone. The first Anasazi residents constructed pit houses on both sides of the wash between AD 500 and 750. During the height of the Chaco culture, from AD 900 to 1115, the "Great Houses"—their purpose still veiled in mystery—were built on the canyon floor and surrounding cliffs.

ROADS LINKING PEOPLE AND SPIRIT

The extensive network of roadways emanating from Chaco bound the constellation of communities—called outliers—throughout the San Juan Basin to the hub of their universe. For all their presumed practicality as trade arteries, the roads nevertheless seem massively overengineered. Why would the Anasazi expend the countless man-hours required to grade 30-foot-wide roadbeds when they had neither draft animals nor the wheel? And why build them arrow-straight up, over, and through intervening terrain rather than follow the path of least resistance?

Dabney Ford, the U.S. Park Service archaeologist at Chaco, draws parallels with the modern Pueblo Indian world, where civil authority, commerce, and theology are all inextricably intertwined. She infers that the Anasazi, like their present-day descendants, would not have undertaken a major public works project like the roads for one purpose alone.

Certainly the roads facilitated centralized management of the widely separated outliers and expedited the movement of goods to and from the canyon, but Ford theorizes that the arteries may have been designed as much for spiritual as for corporeal traffic.

Barely visible troughs of the Chacoan road system, bisected by a modern Park Service road, radiate from Pueblo Alto, a Great House commanding the high ground north of the canyon.

Anasazi pilgrims and traders—or the souls of the departed, according to archaeologist Dabney Ford's interpretation—heading south from Pueblo Alto to Chaco Canyon's north rim and Pueblo Bonito used this spacious thoroughfare. Where the road seems to plunge over the precipice, a stairway—much like the one at left, part of another nearby road—helped mortal travelers journeying on foot negotiate the rugged escarpment.

Chetro Ketl (right), *as large as two city blocks, skirts the canyon's northern cliff face. Constructed in 15 separate stages over a period of more than 100 years, this Great House consumed an estimated 50 million pieces of sandstone, each individually cut and dressed to fit. The small kivas* (above) *are integral architectural components of the pueblo. In the large photo, an open plaza connects the main complex with the Great Kiva* (lower left), *which measures 60 feet in diameter.*

THE UBIQUITOUS KIVA: TEMPLE AND TOWN HALL

Reinforcing the notion that the Great Houses in Chaco fulfilled a ceremonial role is the large number of kivas found in and around them. Chetro Ketl, one of the grandest pueblos in the canyon, contains many small kivas within its walls. Some of its original kivas were backfilled by the Anasazi as they altered and expanded the pueblo during Chaco's heyday.

In the 1920s and 1930s, the archaeologist Edgar L. Hewett undertook a long-term study of Chetro Ketl. After excavating part of the pueblo itself, his team began to dig in the plaza facing the front wall. Beneath the smooth surface they discovered kiva after kiva "crowding, cutting into, and overlying one another." All were circular and masonry lined, but "no two are alike in all respects," Hewett reported. "There is something to keep the archaeologist guessing every day."

Also within the plaza lay a sizable depression in the sandy soil. "It proved to be one of the surprises that we look for in the Chaco," he wrote, "an enormous circular ceremonial structure." In this subterranean chamber, called a Great Kiva, members of the community could gather to discuss secular matters or hold sacred rituals.

One of Chaco Canyon's largest, the Great Kiva at Chetro Ketl contains four circular holes in its floor to hold massive wooden roof supports. Sandstone disks, which served as footings, have been removed from the holes. The square masonry form at the center is a firebox.

whole logs, cut with stone axes on forested mountains up to 50 miles distant, served as floor and roof supports for the multistory pueblos. Archaeologists estimate that 215,000 trees were felled to construct the Great Houses.

SHRINES OF STONE
BUILT TO LAST

Over the course of the two-century building surge that produced the Great Houses, Anasazi masons employed several different methods. The finest stonework in the canyon is in a style labeled "distinctively Chacoan." The walls consist of a rubble core—randomly shaped chunks of stone bonded with mud mortar—up to three feet thick at the base and tapering inward for the upper stories. A veneer of sandstone blocks covers this core on both the interior and exterior facing.

In early examples of this style, the sandstone was crudely cut and haphazardly fitted together. Later on, however, the Anasazi displayed their impressive mastery of the mason's craft, using stone tools to dress the blocks painstakingly and lay them in coursed rows of alternating sizes. It is obvious from the care invested in these works that enormous expenditures of time and labor were no object to the builders in their pursuit of the aesthetic.

The Anasazi concealed this magnificent stonework under a coating of mud plaster inside and out, perhaps to protect the walls' crumbly mortar from the elements. On all but a handful of protected interior surfaces this layer has worn away, revealing once more the beauty that lies beneath. Many of the walls themselves still stand, an enduring testimony to their builders' workmanship and artistry.

The northeast arc of Pueblo Bonito still rises four stories high in places. Rectangular openings provided light and ventilation to the rooms on the lower levels. The three circular holes once held wooden beams that have since rotted away.

One unusual feature of Chacoan architecture is the shape and position of some of the doorways. The wooden floor beneath the corner door above has collapsed. The T-shaped opening below may have had a mat curtain that could be opened in summer and closed in winter to retain heat.

Pueblo Bonito's designers displayed a remarkable understanding of passive solar heating and cooling techniques. The thick masonry walls—pierced by only a few small windows and doors—mitigate Chaco's wildly fluctuating temperatures, keeping the rooms comfortable even in the stifling summer heat. Oriented to face south, the multistory complex is stepped down from rear to front, creating rooftop terraces and giving each level the maximum benefit of the winter sun.

Despite its ruined state—and extensive damage to the rear wall from a 20th-century rockfall—Pueblo Bonito remains the jewel in the Chacoan crown.

AN EFFLORESCENCE OF NORTH AMERICAN CULTURES

The first inhabitants of the Western Hemisphere arrived from Asia during the last Ice Age via a temporary land bridge across the Bering Sea. Pursuing the big game that provided the bulk of their food supply, these roving hunters—known to archaeologists as Paleo-Indians—had, by about 11,000 BC, fanned out over all the North American continent.

In the vast forest that evolved during the Archaic Period from about 8000 to 1000 BC and stretched from the Great Plains to the Atlantic Ocean and from Hudson Bay to the Gulf of Mexico, a gradual change to a more sedentary way of life occurred.

So rich in edible wild plants, fish, fowl, and game was this region that the Archaic Indians could live off its abundance without constantly moving from site to site as their nomadic ancestors had.

By 1000 BC, a new cultural lifestyle—known as the Woodland Tradition—began to take shape, marked by three innovations that proved crucial to the development of the Mound Builder societies: The Indians began actively cultivating some food crops, they invented pottery, and they devoted much care and ceremony to the burial of their dead.

ADENA
500 BC-AD 1

SANDSTONE TABLET

First of the great Mound Builders, the Adena culture emerged in the fertile Ohio Valley and spread its influence up and down that river and its tributaries. As the culture developed, burial practices—and the grave goods that accompanied the dead, such as the tablet above—became increasingly more elaborate. Simple, shallow pits were later supplanted by log-lined tombs, but all were covered by mounds of earth. Typically, the Adena added burials to existing mounds, enlarging them layer by layer, thus giving archaeologists a sequential picture of the culture spanning centuries within the same mound. There are an estimated 300 to 500 burial mounds in the Adena heartland. The Adena culture peaked around 100 BC and then, for reasons unknown, began to decline, fading into obscurity by the first century AD.

HOPEWELL
100 BC-AD 400

MICA HAND

Archaeological evidence points to the appearance of a new culture, known as the Hopewell, in Ohio starting around 100 BC. The Hopewell incorporated many traits and customs of the Adena, elevating them to new heights. They built more imposing burial mounds, which contain a greater assortment of regal objects to sustain the deceased. Hopewell grave goods reveal the existence of a trade network that extended far beyond the actual range of the culture's predominance. Shells from the Gulf Coast, copper from the Great Lakes, and mica (*above*) from the southern Appalachians have all been found in Hopewell mounds. Their earthworks, too, went well beyond simple burial mounds. Vast enclosures of packed soil with geometrically precise boundaries dot the landscape of southern Ohio. Some scholars believe these served as ceremonial meeting places for residents of nearby farming hamlets. Between AD 300 and 400, the Hopewell, like the Adena, gradually waned, leaving archaeologists with some theories, numerous artifacts, but many more unanswered questions.

MISSISSIPPIAN
AD 800-1500

FUNERARY POT

For the four centuries following the decline of the Hopewell, the Eastern Woodlands experienced a period of increasing population pressure and readjustment. Around AD 800, a new culture emerged, so distinct from its predecessors that it can be called a tradition in its own right, the Mississippian. Large communities grew up, which probably required more centralized authority—a chief and a rigid hierarchy of lesser nobles below him. The Mississippian realm eventually encompassed much of the eastern United States and left a lasting imprint on the landscape. Huge, flat-topped pyramid mounds—foundations for chiefly dwellings and religious temples—mark the major settlements. The Mississippian Tradition also generated an extraordinary flowering of artistic expression. Incised conch-shell cups, gorgets, and beads; copper objects, stone sculpture, and pottery, like the distinctive human-head effigy vessel shown above, have been unearthed in great numbers from the graves of high-ranking individuals.

The Southwest encompasses a broad, diverse spectrum of terrain. The common denominator is its relative aridity and marginal capacity to support humans in large numbers. Unlike their counterparts in the Eastern Woodlands, the Indians of this region depended to a greater degree on agriculture in adapting from the nomadic hunter-gatherer lifestyle of the Paleo-Indian Period to a sedentary one. During the Archaic Period, increased population levels and a concurrent decrease in surface water forced the people of this region to focus on using local resources to provide adequate sustenance. Three major—and several minor—cultures appeared at roughly the same time. Each made the most of its particular environmental conditions to store sufficient food resources seasonally, creating free time to pursue communal and artistic activities. Ironically, the same climatic conditions that made life so rigorous for the people ensured that the traces of their cultures would survive remarkably intact for modern archaeologists to scrutinize.

HOHOKAM
AD 200-1450

HUMAN EFFIGY VESSEL

Centered in the southern Arizona desert along the Gila and Snake rivers, the Hohokam were skilled agriculturalists, diverting river water into elaborate irrigation systems and obtaining substantial harvests from the parched landscape. Hundreds of miles of canals—excavated from the desert with stone and wooden tools—once laced their homeland. Hohokam artistic achievements are equally impressive. They carved stone palettes in the form of snakes, toads, and birds, molded clay figurines *(above)*, and produced distinctive red-on-buff pottery. They also invented the process of acid etching—on shells from the Gulf of California—centuries before the technique was developed in Renaissance Europe. The causes of the decline of the Hohokam remain obscure, but recent studies indicate that an excess of that most precious commodity, water, might have done them in. Large-scale flooding of the region's rivers could have demolished their unlined irrigation canals and caused a breakdown in the agricultural system.

MOGOLLON
AD 200-1450

MIMBRES BOWL

The Mogollon culture extends from the Arizona-New Mexico border—and the mountain range for which it is named—into northern Mexico, an area far richer in plant and animal life than the desert domain of the Hohokam. By around AD 200, farming was well established and cultural styles became distinctive. As they evolved, the Mogollon abandoned their semisubterranean pit houses and eventually constructed multi-room housing units called pueblos. They also built rectangular ceremonial structures, called kivas. One branch of the Mogollon, called the Mimbres, are best known today for their artistic achievements in ceramics. The striking pottery *(above)* is widely acclaimed for its extraordinary quality and detail. There is no archaeological evidence of a hierarchical social structure among the Mogollon; no high-ranking burials or caches of luxury goods have ever been found. Around 1200, the Mogollon began to lose their distinctiveness as a culture and, by 1450, had faded away. They are considered the ancestors of the modern western Pueblo Indians.

ANASAZI
AD 200-1450

CHACOAN STYLE PITCHER

The Anasazi occupied the largest parcel of territory, a rugged high tableland marked by extremes in climate and terrain. The earliest Anasazi, who emerged as an identifiable culture around AD 200, lived in pit houses and are known as the Basket Makers for the exquisite quality of their woven containers. Later they developed pottery and moved above ground. Their descendants created the multistory stone pueblos and cliff dwellings that stand today as monuments to their architectural skill. Between AD 1000 and 1300, the culture reached its zenith. Plain and simply painted pottery had been supplanted by intricate works of art, like the pitcher above. Then, for perhaps a number of reasons—climatic change, environmental degradation, or possibly even social friction—the Anasazi world contracted. Ancestral sites were abandoned and people moved on to other locales, creating new pueblos during the 14th and 15th centuries. But the Anasazi, like all the cultures described here, would soon undergo a wrenching ordeal at the hands of a new culture—the Europeans.

ACKNOWLEDGMENTS

The editors wish to thank the following for their valuable assistance in the preparation of this volume: Dirk Bakker, Detroit Institute of Arts, Detroit; Kathleen Baxter, National Museum of Natural History, Smithsonian Institution, Washington, D.C.; Robert E. Bell, Norman, Oklahoma; Joseph Bisselle, Oxon Hill, Maryland; T. Bundy, Arizona State Museum, Tucson; Chester Cowlin, Oklahoma Historical Society, Oklahoma City; Warren Cremer, Time Expeditions, Sedona, Arizona; Nina Cummings, Field Museum of Natural History, Chicago; Rinita A. Dalan, Southern Illinois University, Edwardsville; Mary Kay Davies, Anthropological Branch Library, Smithsonian Institution, Washington, D.C.; Jeffrey Dean, University of Arizona, Tucson; Rod Dresser, Ansel Adams Publishing Rights Trust, Carmel, California; Julie Droke, Oklahoma Museum of Natural History, Norman; Tom Durant, Harpers Ferry Center, Harpers Ferry, West Virginia; Linda Farnsworth, Coconino National Forest, Flagstaff, Arizona; Sylvia Flowers, Ocmulgee National Monument, Macon, Georgia; Dabney Ford, Chaco Culture National Historical Park, Bloomfield, New Mexico; Melvin Fowler, University of Wisconsin, Milwaukee; Judith Franke, Dickson Mounds Museum, Lewistown, Illinois; Jon Gibson, University of Southwestern Louisiana, Lafayette; Tauni Graham, Ohio Historical Society, Columbus; Alan Harn, Dickson Mounds Museum, Lewistown, Illinois; Robert C. Heyder, Mesa Verde National Park, Colorado; George R. Holley, Southern Illinois University, Edwardsville; Charles Hudson, University of Georgia, Athens; Ramona Hutchinson, Mesa Verde National Park, Colorado; William Iseminger, Cahokia Mounds Historic Site, Collinsville, Illinois; Marvin Jeter, Arkansas Archaeological Survey, Fayetteville; Krisztina Kosse, University of New Mexico, Albuquerque; Martha Labell, Harvard University, Cambridge, Massachusetts; Clark Larsen, Purdue University, West Lafayette, Indiana; Diana Leonard, University of Colorado Museum, Boulder; Ed Lyon, Metairie, Louisiana; Robert Mainfort, Memphis State University, Memphis, Tennessee; Jerald T. Milanich, Florida State Museum of Natural History, Gainesville; Phil Newkumet, Norman, Oklahoma; Arthur Olivas, Museum of New Mexico, Santa Fe; Nicholas J. Parella, Smithsonian Institution, Washington, D.C.; Peter Pilles, Coconino National Forest, Flagstaff, Arizona; Mary Lucas Powell, University of Kentucky, Lexington; Mason Rumney III, West Sedona, Arizona; Mary Elizabeth Ruwell, National Anthropological Archives, Smithsonian Institution, Washington, D.C.; Polly and Curtis Schaafsma, Santa Fe, New Mexico; Douglas Schwartz, Santa Fe, New Mexico; Thomas Sever, National Space Technology Laboratory, NSTL Station, Mississippi; Duane Smith, Fort Lewis College, Durango, Colorado; Judy Steiner, Colorado History Museum, Denver; Andrea Stillman, Ansel Adams Publishing Rights Trust, Carmel, California; William Sweetland, Bandelier National Monument, Los Alamos, New Mexico; Scott Travis, Canyon de Chelly National Monument, Chinle, Arizona; Sharron G. Uhler, Colorado Springs Pioneers Museum, Colorado Springs; Ray A. Williamson, Annapolis, Maryland; Pamela Wintle, Museum of Natural History, Smithsonian Institution, Washington, D.C.; Miles Wright, University of Tennessee, Knoxville.

PICTURE CREDITS

BOOKS

Adams, Ansel, with Mary Street Alinder. *Ansel Adams*. Boston: Little, Brown, 1985.

Ambler, J. Richard. *The Anasazi*. Flagstaff: Museum of Northern Arizona Press, 1989.

Amsden, Charles Avery. *Prehistoric Southwesterners from Basketmaker to Pueblo*. Los Angeles: Southwest Museum, 1949.

Anderson, Douglas, and Barbara Anderson. *Chaco Canyon*. Tucson: Southwest Parks and Monuments Association, 1981.

Bandelier, Adolf F. *The Delight Makers*. San Diego: Harcourt Brace Jovanovich, 1971.

Barnes, F. A., and Michaelene Pendleton. *Canyon Country Prehistoric Indians*. Salt Lake City: Wasatch Publishers, 1979.

Barnett, Franklin. *Dictionary of Prehistoric Indian Artifacts of the American Southwest*. Flagstaff, Ariz.: Northland Publishing, 1973.

Barry, Patricia. *Bandelier National Monument*. Tucson: Southwest Parks and Monuments Association, 1990.

Brody, J. J.:
The Anasazi. New York: Rizzoli, 1990.
Anasazi and Pueblo Painting. Albuquerque: University of New Mexico Press, 1991.

Brody, J. J., Catherine J. Scott, and Steven A. LeBlanc. *Mimbres Pottery*. New York: Hudson Hills Press, 1983.

Brose, David S., James A. Brown, and David W. Penney. *Ancient Art of the American Woodland Indians*. New York: Harry N. Abrams, 1985.

Brose, David S., and N'omi Greber (Eds.). *Hopewell Archaeology*. Kent, Ohio: Kent State University Press, 1979.

Caldwell, Joseph R., and Robert L. Hall (Eds.). *Hopewellian Studies* (Scientific Papers, Vol. 12). Springfield: Illinois State Museum, 1977.

Ceram, C. W. *The First American*. New York: Harcourt Brace Jovanovich, 1971.

Coe, Michael, Dean Snow, and Elizabeth Benson. *Atlas of Ancient America*. New York: Facts On File Publications, 1986.

Cohen, Mark Nathan, and George J. Armelagos (Eds.). *Paleopathology at the Origins of Agriculture*. Orlando, Fla.: Academic Press, 1984.

Contributions from the Museum of the American Indian, Heye Foundation (Vol. 14). New York: Museum of the American Indian, Heye Foundation, 1945.

Cordell, Linda S. *Prehistory of the Southwest*. San Diego: Academic Press, 1984.

Cordell, Linda S., and George J. Gumerman (Eds.). *Dynamics of Southwest Prehistory*. Washington, D.C.: Smithsonian Institution Press, 1989.

Dragoo, Don W. *Mounds for the Dead*. Pittsburgh: Carnegie Museum of Natural History, 1989.

Fagan, Brian M.:
Ancient North America. London: Thames and Hudson, 1991.
In the Beginning (6th ed.). Boston: Scott, Foresman, 1988.

Ferguson, William M., and Arthur H. Rohn. *Anasazi Ruins of the Southwest in Color*. Albuquerque: University of New Mexico Press, 1990.

Fewkes, Jesse Walter. *The Mimbres: Art and Archaeology*. Albuquerque: Avanyu Publishing, 1990.

Fish, Paul R., and Suzanne K. Fish. "Hohokam Political and Social Organization." In *Exploring the Hohokam*, edited by George J. Gumerman. Albuquerque: University of New Mexico Press, 1991.

Flint, Richard, and Shirley Cushing Flint. *A Pocket Guide to Chaco Canyon Architecture*. Villanueva, N. Mex.: Richard and Shirley Flint, 1987.

Fowler, Melvin L. *The Cahokia Atlas*. Springfield: Illinois Historic Preservation Agency, 1989.

Frazier, Kendrick. *People of Chaco*. New York: W. W. Norton, 1986.

Fundaburk, Emma Lila, and Mary Douglass Fundaburk Foreman (Eds.). *Sun Circles and Human Hands*. Luverne, Ala.: Emma Lila Fundaburk, 1957.

Gilbert, Robert I., Jr., and James H. Mielke (Eds.). *The Analysis of Prehistoric Diets*. Orlando, Fla.: Academic Press, 1985.

Griffin, James B. "Changing Concepts of the Prehistoric Mississippian Cultures of the Eastern United States" (Chap. 2, Part 1 of *Alabama and the Borderlands*, edited by R. Reid Badger and Lawrence A. Clayton). University: University of Alabama Press, 1985.

Gumerman, George J. (Ed.). *Exploring the Hohokam*. Albuquerque: University of New Mexico Press, 1991.

Hudson, Charles. *The Southeastern Indians*. Knoxville: University of Tennessee Press, 1976.

Jackson, Clarence S. *Picture Maker of the Old West: William H. Jackson*. New York: Charles Scribner's Sons, 1947.

Jackson, William Henry. *Time Exposure*. New York: G. P. Putnam's Sons, 1940.

Jennings, Jesse D. *Prehistory of North America*. Mountain View, Calif.: Mayfield Publishing, 1989.

Jones, William C., and Elizabeth B. Jones (Comps.). *William Henry Jackson's Colorado*. Boulder, Colo.: Pruett Publishing, 1975.

Kopper, Philip, and the Editors of Smithsonian Books. *The Smithsonian Book of North American Indians: Before the Com-*

ing of the Europeans. Washington, D.C.: Smithsonian Books, 1986.

Lange, Frederick W. *Cortez Crossroads*. Boulder, Colo.: Johnson Books, 1989.

Lekson, Stephen H. *Great Pueblo Architecture of Chaco Canyon, New Mexico*. Albuquerque: University of New Mexico Press, 1989.

Lister, Robert H., and Florence C. Lister:
Archaeology and Archaeologists: Chaco Canyon. Albuquerque: University of New Mexico Press, 1981.
Mesa Verde National Park. Mancos, Colo.: ARA Mesa Verde, 1987.
Those Who Came Before. Globe, Ariz.: Southwest Parks and Monuments Association, 1983.

McAdams, William. *Records of Ancient Races in the Mississippi Valley*. St. Louis: C. R. Barns Publishing, 1887.

McNitt, Frank. *Richard Wetherill Anasazi*. Albuquerque: University of New Mexico Press, 1966.

Matlock, Gary. *Enemy Ancestors*. Flagstaff, Ariz.: Northland Publishing, 1988.

Mays, Buddy. *Ancient Cities of the Southwest*. San Francisco: Chronicle Books, 1990.

Michael, Henry N., and Elizabeth K. Ralph (Eds.). *Dating Techniques for the Archaeologist*. Cambridge: MIT Press, 1971.

Morgan, William N. *Prehistoric Architecture in the Eastern United States*. Cambridge: MIT Press, 1980.

The Mural Project: Photography by Ansel Adams. Selected by Peter Wright and John Armor. Santa Barbara, Calif.: Reverie Press, 1989.

Noble, David Grant. *Ancient Ruins of the Southwest*. Flagstaff, Ariz.: Northland Publishing, 1981.

Noble, David Grant (Ed.):
The Hohokam. Santa Fe, N. Mex.: School of American Research Press, 1991.
New Light on Chaco Canyon. Santa Fe, N. Mex.: School of American Research Press, 1984.

Nordenskiöld, Gustav. *The Cliff Dwellers of the Mesa Verde*. Translated by D. Lloyd Morgan. Chicago: P. A. Norstedt & Söner, 1893.

Palmer, Edward. *Edward Palmer's Arkansaw Mounds*. Edited by Marvin D. Jeter. Fayetteville: University of Arkansas Press, 1990.

Phillips, Philip, and James A. Brown. *Pre-Columbian Shell Engravings*. Cambridge, Mass.: Peabody Museum Press, 1978.

Renfrew, Colin, and Paul Bahn. *Archaeology*. New York: Thames and Hudson, 1991.

Rose, Martin R., Jeffrey S. Dean, and William J. Robinson. *The Past Climate* of Arroyo Hondo, New Mexico, Reconstructed from Tree Rings. Santa Fe, N. Mex.: School of American Research Press, 1981.

Schaafsma, Polly. Indian Rock Art of the Southwest. Albuquerque: University of New Mexico Press, 1990.

Sever, Thomas L. "Remote Sensing." Chap. 14 in Benchmarks in Time and Culture, edited by Joel F. Drinkard, Jr., Gerald L. Mattingly, and J. Maxwell Miller. Atlanta: Scholars Press, 1988.

Silverberg, Robert. Mound Builders of Ancient America. Greenwich, Conn.: New York Graphic Society, 1968.

Smith, Bruce D.:
"Agricultural Chiefdoms of the Eastern Woodlands." Chap. 5 in The Cambridge History of the Native Peoples of the Americas, North America (Vol. 1), edited by Bruce Trigger and Wilcomb Washburn (in press).
"Mississippian Elites and Solar Alignments: A Reflection of Managerial Necessity, or Levers of Social Inequality?" In Lords of the Southeast. Washington, D.C.: American Anthropological Society, 1991.
"Mississippian Patterns of Subsistence and Settlement." Chap. 3 in Alabama and the Borderlands, edited by R. Reid Badger and Lawrence A. Clayton. Tuscaloosa: University of Alabama Press, 1985.
"The Temple Mound Builders." In The American Land. New York: W. W. Norton, 1979.

Smith, Duane A. Mesa Verde National Park. Lawrence: University Press of Kansas, 1988.

Squier, E. G., and E. H. Davis. Ancient Monuments of the Mississippi Valley: Comprising the Results of Extensive Original Surveys and Explorations. New York: AMS Press, 1973.

Steponaitis, Vincas P. "Location Theory and Complex Chiefdoms: A Mississippian Example." Chap. 14 in Mississippian Settlement Patterns, edited by Bruce D. Smith. New York: Academic Press, 1978.

Stuart, Gene S. America's Ancient Cities. Washington, D.C.: National Geographic Society, 1988.

Supplee, Charles, Douglas Anderson, and Barbara Anderson. Canyon de Chelly. Las Vegas, Nev.: KC Publications, 1990.

Thomas, Cyrus. Report on the Mound Explorations of the Bureau of Ethnology. Washington, D.C.: Smithsonian Institution Press, 1985.

Viele, Catherine W. Voices in the Canyon. Globe, Ariz.: Southwest Parks and Monuments Association, 1980.

Watson, Don. Indians of the Mesa Verde.

Mesa Verde National Park, Colo.: Mesa Verde Museum Association, n.d.

Webb, William S., and Charles E. Snow. The Adena People. Knoxville: University of Tennessee Press, 1974.

Wenger, Gilbert R. The Story of Mesa Verde National Park. Mesa Verde National Park, Colo.: Mesa Verde Museum Association, 1991.

Williamson, Ray A. Living the Sky. Boston: Houghton Mifflin, 1984.

Woodward, Susan L., and Jerry N. McDonald. Indian Mounds of the Middle Ohio Valley. Blacksburg, Va.: McDonald & Woodward Publishing, 1986.

PERIODICALS

Beans, Bruce E. "Why? Chaco Fever." Philadelphia Inquirer Magazine, June 9, 1991.

Canby, Thomas Y. "The Anasazi." National Geographic, November 1982.

Cordell, Linda S. "Why Did They Leave and Where Did They Go?" Exploration (Annual Bulletin of the School of American Research), 1985.

Dexter, Ralph W. "F. W. Putnam at the Serpent Mound in Adams County, Ohio." Journal of the Steward Anthropological Society, Fall/Spring 1988-89.

Douglass, Andrew Ellicott. "The Secret of the Southwest Solved by Talkative Tree Rings." National Geographic, December 1929.

Fish, Paul R. "Prehistoric Land Use in the Perkinsville Valley." Arizona Archaeologist, January 1974.

Gibson, Jon L. "Earth Sitting: Architectural Masses at Poverty Point, Northeastern Louisiana." Louisiana Archaeology, November 13, 1986.

Haury, Emil W., and Helga Teiwes. "First Masters of the American Desert." National Geographic, May 1967.

Hayes, Alden C. "Mesa Verde: A Century of Research." Exploration (Annual Bulletin of the School of American Research), 1985.

Ina, Lauren. "Indian Burial Site Focus of Controversy." Washington Post, November 10, 1991.

Joyce, Christopher. "Archaeology Takes to the Skies." New Scientist, January 25, 1992.

Larsen, Clark Spencer:
"Bioarchaeological Interpretations of Subsistence Economy and Behavior from Human Skeletal Remains." Advances in Archaeological Method and Theory, 1987, Vol. 10.
"Telltale Bones." Archaeology, March/April 1992.

Lekson, Stephen H., et al. "The Chaco Canyon Community." Scientific American, July 1988.

Pilles, Peter J., Jr. "The Southern Sinagua." Plateau, 1981, Vol. 53, no. 1.

Rensberger, Boyce. "Placing Man in America 28,000 Years Ago." Washington Post, February 10, 1992.

Rohn, Arthur H. "Prehistoric Developments in the Mesa Verde Region." Exploration (Annual Bulletin of the School of American Research), 1985.

Wilford, John Noble. "Lofty Instruments Discern Traces of Ancient Peoples." New York Times, March 10, 1992.

OTHER SOURCES

Bradley, Zorro A. "Canyon de Chelly." Booklet. Washington, D.C.: U.S. National Park Service, 1973.

Chapman, Jefferson. "Tellico Archaeology: 12,000 Years of Native American History." Publications in Anthropology no. 41. Tennessee Valley Authority, 1985.

"Coconino National Forest." Draft interpretive trail guide. Washington, D.C.: U.S. National Park Service, n.d.

"The Dickson Mounds Controversy." Video produced by James Green with WILL TV/Channel 12, October 1991.

"Dickson Mounds Museum." Pamphlet. Illinois State Museum, n.d.

Galloway, Patricia (Ed.). "The Southeastern Ceremonial Complex." Catalog by David H. Dye and Camille Wharey. Lincoln: University of Nebraska Press, 1989.

Griffin, James B. "Cahokia Interaction with Southeastern and Eastern Contemporary Societies." Paper presented at symposium Exploring and Exploding Myths about Cahokia, April 24-28, 1991, New Orleans, La.

Holley, George R., Rinita A. Dalan, and Philip A. Smith. "Investigations in the Cahokia Site Grand Plaza." Manuscript. Edwardsville: Southern Illinois University, May 3, 1991.

Jones, Dewitt, and Linda S. Cordell. "Anasazi World." Catalog. Portland, Ore.: Graphic Arts Center Publishing, 1985.

Murphy, Dan. "Bandelier, the Man." Transcript of speech commemorating the 100th anniversary of A. Bandelier's first visit to Frijoles Canyon, delivered October 16, 1990.

Smith, Bruce D. "Hopewellian Farmers of Eastern North America." Paper presented at 11th Congress, International Union of Prehistoric and Protohistoric Sciences, September 1-6, 1987, Mainz, Germany.

Wymer, Dee Anne. "The Paleoethnobotanical Record of Central Ohio—100 B.C. to A.D. 800: Subsistence Continuity amid Cultural Change." Dissertation. Columbus: Ohio State University, 1987.

ROCKY MOUNTAINS

Great Salt Lake

PICTOGRAPHS

• Grand Gulch

Mesa Verde •

Little Colorado River

Chaco Canyon •

Arkansas River

TURQUOISE
BASKET

Colorado River

STONE
PALETTE

Gila River

Snaketown

MIMBRES VALLEY

MIMBRES
POTTERY

PACIFIC OCEAN

• Casas Grandes

FEMALE EFFIGY
VESSEL

Rio Grande